in English

5

Third Edition

Michael Walker

Addison-Wesley Publishing Company
Reading, Massachusetts • Menlo Park, California • New York
Don Mills, Ontario • Wokingham, England • Amsterdam • Bonn
Singapore • Sydney • Tokyo • Madrid • San Juan

A Publication of the World Language Division

Director of Product Development: Judith Bittinger
Project Director: Elinor Chamas
Editorial: Kathleen Sands Boehmer
Manufacturing/Production: James W. Gibbons
Text Design: John F. Kelly
Cover Design: Don Taka
Illustrations: Marcy Ramsey, Walter Fournier, Akihito Shirakawa, Frank Bolle Jr.
Art Direction: Publishers' Graphics

Photo Credits: p. 1, A and A Limousine Renting, Inc., Big Surf, Tempe, Arizona; p. 3, Bruce Anderson; p. 24, Owen Franken/Stock Boston; p. 25, Movie Star News, Alaska Historical Society, Skinner Collection; p. 30, Bruce Anderson; p. 49, Bruce Anderson, Marshall Henrichs; p. 70, Anestis Diakopolous/Stock Boston; p. 73, Movie Star News, Institut d'Information et de Documentation, Brussels; p. 74, Bruce Anderson, p. 89, Bruce Anderson; p. 97, Bruce Anderson, United Press International; p. 120, N.Y. Convention and Visitors Bureau.

Acknowledgements: pp. 68–69, "The Unknown Citizen" from *W.H. Auden: Collected Poems,* ed. by Edward Mendelson. Copyright © 1976 by Edward Mendelson, William Meredith & Monroe K. Spears, Executors of the Estate of W.H. Auden. Reprinted by permission of Random House, Inc. and Faber and Faber, Ltd.; pp. 92–93, "The Sound of Silence" Copyright © 1964 by Paul Simon. Used by permission of the Publisher.; pp. 116–117, "Confessions of a Born Spectator" reprinted by permission of Curtis Brown, Ltd. Copyright © 1937 by Ogden Nash.

ISBN: 0-201-53516-5
1 2 3 4 5 6 7 8 9 10 -VH- 96 95 94 93 92 91

Introduction

NEW HORIZONS IN ENGLISH is a communication-based, six-level, basal series planned and written to make the learning of English as a second language effective and rewarding. Stimulating opportunities to practice listening, speaking, reading, and writing skills develop independence and confidence in the use of English. Thoughtfully chosen vocabulary gives students the words they need to communicate in their new language in a variety of situations; carefully paced introduction of grammatical and structural concepts helps insure a strong foundation of communication skills.

Important to every learner is a sense of achievement, a feeling that he or she has successfully accomplished the tasks presented. Motivation, the desire to learn, is equally important. NEW HORIZONS IN ENGLISH is written to satisfy both needs: to provoke, through selection of topics, vocabulary, and illustrations, a genuine interest in learning more, and to pace and schedule material in such a way that achievement and mastery are facilitated.

The language used in NEW HORIZONS IN ENGLISH is contemporary and relevant. Most important, it is English that students can and will use outside the classroom. Natural exchanges and dialogues arise from the real-life situations that form unit themes. New to this edition is the addition of literature, with selections that will increase students' enjoyment of the language. Also, students will be challenged by the "Fast Track" pages in which new and varied material is presented.

The emphasis on speaking and listening, with meaning always paramount, means that oral communicative competence develops early and is broadened and deepened as students move through the series. Parallel development of reading and writing skills promotes competence in other communication areas at the same time.

Dialogues and readings from the texts, and many of the exercises, are recorded on the optional tape cassette program, which provides models of American pronunciation and intonation.

A complete program to build communicative competence, NEW HORIZONS IN ENGLISH provides motivation, mastery, and a sense of achievement. Every student—and every teacher—needs the feeling of pride in a job well done. NEW HORIZONS IN ENGLISH, with its unbeatable formula for classroom success, insures that this need will be filled.

Contents

Expressing: logical conclusions/deductions, personal information

Poem: "The Unknown Citizen" by W.H. Auden
Content reading: industrial pollution

use of indefinite articles with place names it is **vs.** there is/there are
it in statements about weather, distance, weight and length
similes as . . . as
nouns as adjectives
review: noun modifiers, reported speech, compound words, genitive forms: noun +'s/s'

1

What do you think you'll be reading about in this unit?

Partner Practice

—Dick drove to the **library**, didn't he?
—No, he didn't.
—Where *did* he drive?
—He drove to the **park.**

—Did they build **a factory**?
—No, they didn't.
—Well, what *did* they build?
—They built **a hotel.**

 Now use the pictures and other places you know to make dialogues of your own.

MEMORY BANK		
factory	stadium	drugstore
library	park	hotel
office	hospital	bank

—Did you eat all the **bread**?
—No, I ate all the **nuts**, though.
—And did you drink all the **coffee**?
—No, but I drank all the **milk**!

—Did you buy **oranges** on the way home?
—Yes, and I bought **tea**, too.
—Did you forget the **cheese**?
—Yes, I'm sorry. I forgot it.

Now use the pictures and other words you know to make dialogues of your own.

MEMORY BANK

meat	cake	fruit	fish
cookies	nuts	coffee	milk
sandwiches	oranges	tea	cheese

Read & Predict

Every morning at eleven o'clock, a shiny Rolls Royce drove through Central Park in New York City. Inside the car sat a chauffeur and his employer, a well-known millionaire.

Each morning the millionaire noticed a poorly-dressed man sitting on a park bench. The man always sat staring at the 5 luxurious hotel where the millionaire lived. One day, the millionaire was so curious about the man that he ordered his chauffeur to stop the car. He walked to the bench and said to the poor man, "Excuse me, but I just have to know why you sit staring at my hotel every morning." "Sir," said the man, 10 "I'm a failure. I have no money, no family, no home. I sleep on this bench, and every night I dream that one day I'm going to sleep in that hotel."

The millionaire had an idea. He felt very pleased with himself as he said, "Tonight your dream is going to come true. 15 I have paid for the best room in that hotel for you for a whole month." And that is exactly what happened—except for one strange thing.

A few days later, the millionaire went by the man's room to ask him how he was enjoying himself. To his surprise, he 20 found that the man had moved back to his park bench.

 Can you guess why? You'll find our explanation on page 9.

DO YOU REMEMBER?
1. Where did the Rolls Royce drive?
2. Who was in the car?
3. What did the millionaire notice?
4. What did he order his chauffeur to do?
5. What did the millionaire do then?
6. What did the millionaire say to the poor man?
7. What did the poor man answer?
8. What was the millionaire's idea?
9. Why was the millionaire surprised a few days later?

Partner Practice

—**You haven't met the new boss yet, have you?**
—No. Perhaps **I'll meet her** today.

1. They haven't caught the bank robber yet, have they?
2. You haven't spent your birthday check yet, have you?
3. She hasn't swept the floor yet, has she?
4. You haven't found your watch yet, have you?
5. He hasn't made the bookcase yet, has he?

—**I just flew something I've never flown before.**
—Really? What did you **fly?**
—**I flew a plane.**

 You can complete these any way you like!

1. I just drove something I've never driven before.
2. I just ate something . . .
3. I just wrote something . . .
4. I just rode something . . .
5. I just saw something . . .
6. I just drank something . . .
7. I just sewed something . . .

MEMORY BANK	meet	met	met	catch	caught	caught
	spend	spent	spent	sweep	swept	swept
	find	found	found	make	made	made
	write	wrote	written	drive	drove	driven
	eat	ate	eaten	fly	flew	flown
	ride	rode	ridden	see	saw	seen
	drink	drank	drunk	sew	sewed	sewn

—What have you been doing?
—I've been **recording a song.**
Have you ever **recorded** one?
—Yes, I have.
—When did you **record** one?
—I **recorded** one just last week.

1. painting a picture

2. reading a poem

3. making a map

4. building a model

5. writing a story

6. driving a race car

7. eating octopus

8. flying a plane

9. sewing a dress

HOW ABOUT YOU?

1. Have you ever written a story? What was it about?
2. Have you ever built a model or sewn a dress? What did it look like?
3. Have you ever eaten something unusual? Did you like it?
4. What have you been doing lately?

Read & Understand

BIG SURF

When school is over for the day, many students in Tempe, Arizona meet at *Big Surf* for an afternoon of surfing. This may not sound strange to you unless you know that Tempe is in the middle of the desert—more than 400 miles from the
5 Pacific Ocean!

How did surfing in the desert begin? It all began a few years ago when a man named Dexter spent his vacation in California. He found the surfers who rode the big Pacific waves on their surfboards very exciting. Dexter returned
10 to Arizona and began experimenting with model wave-making machines. After several failures, he successfully built a machine that could make four to five foot waves.

Dexter built a lake that holds four million gallons of water. The water is recirculated through a tank and sent
15 through 15 underwater gates. The waves break at one-minute intervals, and surfers can ride them for 430 feet to the end of the lake.

Whole families spend the day at *Big Surf* swimming, surfing, playing ball, eating, drinking, riding in boats, or just enjoying the sun.

DO YOU REMEMBER?

1. Why is surfing in Tempe so strange?
2. What was Dexter excited by on his vacation?
3. How many gallons of water does it hold?
4. How often do the waves break? How long a ride can you get?
5. What else can people do at *Big Surf*?

Listen & Understand

HENRY JOHN KAISER

Listen carefully to the life story of an American millionaire. Decide whether each sentence is true or false; write your answers on a separate piece of paper.

1. Henry John Kaiser was born in New York City.
2. His father had come from Europe.
3. His father was rich.
4. Henry left school when he was twelve.
5. He got married before he was twenty.
6. He built dams.
7. He built a cement factory.
8. The factory today is small, but good.
9. Kaiser had built ships from the very beginning.
10. His company built ships only for the United States.
11. Kaiser was a big, tall man.
12. He weighed more than 240 pounds.
13. He built a hotel for his wife.
14. Kaiser died in his eighties.

RICH MAN, POOR MAN

When the millionaire asked why, the man said, "You see, when I'm down here sleeping on my bench, I dream I'm up there, in that luxurious hotel. It's a wonderful dream. But when I was up there, I dreamed I was back on this cold bench. It was a terrible dream, and I couldn't get any sleep at all!"

Partner Practice

Julio has just moved to his own apartment. His mother has come to visit!

—Look at **these dishes**!
 Haven't you ever **washed them**?
—Of course! I **washed them**
 just last month!

1. ironed

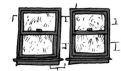

2. cleaned

3. swept

4. watered

5. emptied

6. made

—Have you called Bill?
—Yes, I have.
—What did he say?
—He said that he had just **lost his watch**.

1. seen a movie

2. fallen down

3. found a wallet

4. torn his jacket

5. swum two miles

6. broken his leg

Julio's father has been to see him. Now Julio's mother wants to know all about the visit.

—Did he promise he would **cut his hair**?
—I'm afraid not. He said that he had never **cut** it before, so he wasn't going to **cut** it now.

1. make his bed

2. take his medicine

3. sweep his apartment

4. do his laundry

5. read his mail

6. drink his milk

—Did you **empty the trash** last night?
—I was going to, but Anne had already **emptied** it.

1.

2.

3.

4.

5.

6.

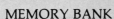

MEMORY BANK

1. wash the car   2. iron my shirt   3. sweep the floor

4. make a cake   5. write the note   6. buy some wine

Read & Predict

THE "LAZYPEEL" PEELER

My friend George Goatman has retired from business. He's bought a house in the country. It's a lonely place, and George hasn't made many friends. He'd rather be alone, anyway. (George has always been a grouch, really!)

Not long ago, George was surprised by a knock on his 5
front door. A salesman from the "Lazypeel" Potato Peeler Company had driven up. "Whatever you're selling, I'm not buying," George growled.

"I've given many demonstrations of our fantastic peeler, sir. And believe me, after you've seen it, you'll want it. Let 10
me demonstrate--free of charge, of course."

The salesman ran out to his car. George didn't want any demonstration. He intended to peel his potatoes with a knife, as he had always done. The salesman, however, didn't give up. He had taken a whole bag of potatoes from the trunk of 15
his car. He carried it into George's kitchen and emptied it into the sink.

"Now, if I don't peel all these potatoes in five minutes, I'll eat my hat!" the salesman promised. "Uh, where's the best place to plug in the peeler?" 20

Now my friend George had begun to enjoy himself. He smiled slowly and said, "I hope you'll enjoy eating your hat!"

Why was Goatman so sure that the salesman wouldn't be able to peel the potatoes in five minutes? You'll find our explanation on page 18.

DO YOU REMEMBER?

1. How do you know that Mr. Goatman's farmhouse was not near any others?
2. How do you know that Mr. Goatman did not work?
3. How do you know that he was not happy to see the salesman?
4. What was the salesman selling?
5. How much was he going to charge for a demonstration?
6. How did the salesman think Mr. Goatman would feel about the peeler?
7. Do you think the salesman sold the peeler to Mr. Goatman? Why or why not?

Partner Practice

—Would you like more cake?

—Yes, I would. Thank you!

—Would you like to play tennis today?

—No, I wouldn't. Sorry.

 Use the pictures and words of your own to make more questions and answers.

—**If I bought a dog, would you be angry?**

—Of course I would./Of course I wouldn't.

1. If I made a cake, would you eat it?
2. If I cut my hair, would you like it?
3. If I gave you ten dollars, would you be happy?
4. If I wrote you a poem, would you be pleased?
5. If I broke the TV, would you fix it?
6. If I paid for the ticket, would you go to the movies?
7. If I bought some milk, would you drink it?
8. If I told a joke, would you laugh?

 If I won $5,000, I would travel around the world. What would you do?

—**Have you taken out the trash yet?**

—No, but I'll **take it out** tonight.

—But you promised that you would **take it out** yesterday!

1. Have you written a letter to your grandmother yet?
2. Have you bought a bed yet?
3. Have you sold your motorcycle yet?
4. Have you sewn your jacket yet?
5. Have you read that book yet?

Here are some inventions that man has made. Look at each of the examples below carefully. Then choose which invention you think each person is talking about.

1. I'm tired of carrying these rocks. I wish somebody would invent . . .

2. I'm tired of rubbing sticks together. I wish somebody would invent . . .

3. I'm tired of these long trips. I wish somebody would invent
. . .

4. I'm tired of reading in this bad light. I wish somebody would invent . . .

5. I'm tired of shouting. I wish somebody would invent . . .

6. I'm tired of freezing at night. I wish somebody would invent
. . .

Read & Understand

A large company has advertised for a male or female to work as an assistant to the head of its Advertising Department. The Personnel Director has interviewed three applicants, and made notes in each interview. Which applicant would you choose? Why?

Appleton, Alice
Female, Age 35
Current Job: Advertising Secretary

1. Has worked for us since 1966; trustworthy and hard working
2. Seems ambitious - interested in better job
3. Knows our business well
4. Current boss (Slater) says: efficient/reliable
5. Has three small children; will work only a few hours of overtime

Banner, Robert
Male, Age 28
Current Job: Teacher

1. Four years at University; well educated
2. Wants to learn more about advertising and how consumers spend their money
3. No business experience, but very good teacher
4. Poised - good speaker
5. Doesn't know much about artists, printing of ads, costs

Carson, Caroline
Female, Age 23
Current Job: Unemployed

1. Just graduated art school; won two prizes
2. Talented - art very good
3. Some good ideas for new TV ads
4. Spent last summer traveling (South America) has lived in London too
5. Perhaps a little too young for Ted's assistant??

DO YOU REMEMBER?

1. What did the company advertise for?
2. Who was interviewing the job applicants?
3. Which of the applicants was already working for the company?
4. Had Robert Banner had any experience working at all?
5. Which applicant wasn't too interested in working overtime?
6. Which applicant was poised? Well-traveled? A good artist? An efficient worker? A good speaker?

Listen & Understand

WANT ADS

Read these ads first. Then listen and decide which person is best for each job.

1. Not exciting, but quiet, regular work. No overtime, only two other people on the staff. Apply in person to Oldtown Cemetery.

2. The government of Transana needs a **SECRETARY** for its Mexican Embassy. Applicants must speak three languages and have several years of experience. Good salary; free maid service. Box 415.

3. OFFICE WORK. Young man or woman looking for summer job or part-time work—this could be your chance. Downtown office. Call 299-5161.

4. TRAVEL AGENCY needs ambitious, pleasant young people to work as guides. Travel to other countries; long hours, but good pay. Some office work. Write Box 314.

5. OFFICE WORK. Mornings only. Intelligent male or female to handle bills, salary checks, orders. Small company outside Dallas. Call 662-4167.

6. Construction Workers: New hotel on coast. Two to three months work. Apply in person, Seacoast Hotel.

1. Job number . . . is the best one for Alice Cooper.
2. Job number . . . is the best one for John Rose.
3. Job number . . . is the best one for Gloria Fernandez.
4. Job number . . . is the best one for Kenneth Wong.
5. Job number . . . is the best one for Joanne Brooks.

Partner Practice

Some words in English have silent letters—letters you don't pronounce, even though you see them. In the words below, the final -e's are silent.

inside	polite	suppose	balance
rule	wave	female	romance
behave	sense	late	page

In this group of words, the -a's are silent, and the -e's sound just like the -e in *pen*.

bread	dead	instead	ready
pleasant	sweater	weather	leather

In this group of words, the -a's are silent too, but the -e's that go before the -a's sound just like the -e in *easy*.

scream	seasick	pleats	cheap
seat	beach	dream	reach

Practice reading these sentences.

1. Please turn to page 110.
2. I really like your new sweater.
3. Bread used to be cheap.
4. The waves were crashing onto the beach.
5. Please come inside and take a seat.
6. Do you dream about pleasant things?

ON YOUR OWN

Now work with a partner and make up sentences of your own. Use the words on this page and other words you know with silent letters. You can write your sentences for extra credit.

THE "LAZYPEELER" PEELER
Mr. Goatman had no electricity.

Ricky is fifteen years old.　　　He's a fifteen-year-old boy.

1. The house has six rooms.　　It's a six-room house.
2. I work seven days a week.　　I work a seven-day week.
3. Mary found five dollars.　　She found a five-dollar bill.
4. Tim worked six hours today.　　He worked a six-hour day.
5. He took a trip for two weeks.　　He took a two-week trip.

Was Marvin fourteen?　　　　(15) No, he was a
　　　　　　　　　　　　　　　　fifteen-year-old boy.

1. Did he build a house with five rooms?　　(7)
2. Did he work four days a week?　　(5)
3. Did he buy a wallet for five dollars?　　(10)
4. Did he rest for two hours?　　(3)
5. Did he take a trip for a week?　　(4)

—**You must have waited for two hours!**
—**I waited** for **two and a half** hours to be exact!

1. You must have slept for an hour!
2. You must have run for four hours!
3. You must have driven for three hours!
4. You must have walked for five hours!

The Mad Gardener's Song

He thought he saw an Elephant,
    That practiced on a fife:
He looked again, and found it was
    A letter from his wife.
"At length I realize," he said,
    "The bitterness of Life!"

He thought he saw a Buffalo
    Upon the chimney-piece:
He looked again, and found it was
    His Sister's Husband's Niece.
"Unless you leave this house," he said,
    "I'll send for the Police!"

He thought he saw a Rattlesnake
    That questioned him in Greek:
He looked again, and found it was
    The Middle of Next Week.
"The one thing I regret," he said,
    "Is that it cannot speak!"

He thought he saw a Banker's Clerk
    Descending from the bus:
He looked again, and found it was
    A Hippopotamus.
"If this should stay to dine," he said,
    "There won't be much for us!"

He thought he saw a Kangaroo
    That worked a coffee-mill:
He looked again, and found it was
    A Vegetable-Pill.
"Were I to swallow this," he said,
    "I should be very ill!"

He thought he saw a Coach-and-Four
    That stood beside his bed:
He looked again, and found it was
    A Bear without a Head.
"Poor thing," he said, "poor silly thing!
    It's waiting to be fed!"

He thought he saw an Albatross
    That fluttered round the lamp:
He looked again, and found it was
    A Penny-Postage-Stamp.
"You'd best be getting home," he said,
    "The nights are very damp!"

He thought he saw a Garden-Door
    That opened with a key:
He looked again, and found it was
    A Double Rule of Three:
"And all its mystery," he said,
    "Is clear as day to me!"

He thought he saw an Argument
    That proved he was the Pope:
He looked again, and found it was
    A Bar of Mottled Soap.
"A fact so dread," he faintly said,
    "Extinguishes all hope!"

Lewis Carroll

Fast Track: *Read and Research*

A WOMEN'S BRIGADE OF TREE PLANTERS

In 1977 Wangari Maathai took on a formidable mission: holding back Kenya's advancing desert. Rampant tree cutting and un-checked population growth have stripped much of the country's land, generating hunger and poverty. In response, Maathai organized the Green Belt Move-ment, a national tree-planting program run by women.

"Because women here are responsible for their children, they cannot sit back, waste time and see them starve," explains Maathai, 49, who was the first Kenyan woman to earn a Ph.D. (in anatomy) and the first to become a professor at the University of Nairobi.

With GBM's support, women establish nurseries within their villages and then persuade farmers to accept and raise tree seedlings. GBM pays the women 2¢ for each native plant they grow; exotic species are worth one-fifth as much. Farmers get the plants for free. So far, Maathai has recruited about 50,000 women, who have spurred the planting of 10 million trees. She still has a long way to go toward her original goal of planting a tree for every Kenyan (the population is now about 24 million), but in the meantime, her idea has inspired similar movements in more than a dozen other African nations.

GREENPEACE

In 1977, Wangari Maathai took things into her own hands and organized the Green Belt Movement. There are, however, a number of international organizations which are concerned with our environment. One of the most well-known of these is an organization called "Greenpeace."

Research Topics

1. Who was the founder of Greenpeace and how or why did this person get the idea?
2. When was Greenpeace founded?
3. Does Greenpeace have a head office? If so, where is it?
4. Does Greenpeace have any "official" or governmental support? If not, where does Greenpeace get its funds from?
5. List some of Greenpeace's greatest successes and failures.

FORESTS

Rampant tree cutting had stripped much of Kenya's land. The same thing is happening in other parts of the world. Why are people so concerned about this?

Research Topics

1. Find an area of the world where forests are in danger. Explain how the forests are threatened.
2. What is the reason for this stripping of the forest? Is it the growth of the population, bad agricultural methods, multinational greed, demands of the developing world, political abuse or some other reason?
3. What can be done to stop the process?
4. Are there any examples of places where the process has been stopped? If so, is there any way of reversing it?

THE UNITED NATIONS

Most, but not all, of the nations of the world are members of the United Nations Organization. What are the aims and ambitions of this organization?

Research Topics

1. When was the United Nations founded?
2. What was the aim of the United Nations?
3. How are decisions made at the United Nations?
4. Do any nations have the power to stop these decisions? How and why?
5. Report on any special or spectacular successes that the United Nations has achieved.
6. What is the future of the United Nations?

What do you think you'll be reading about
in this unit?

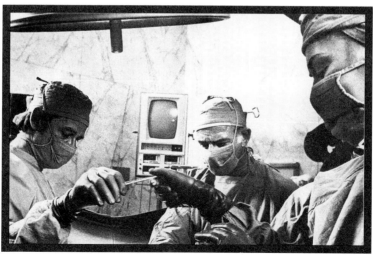

Partner Practice

—Is there any **milk**?
—Yes, there's some in that **bottle**.

1. tea   teapot

2. sugar   sugar bowl

3. salt   salt shaker

4. detergent   box

—Can you think of anything that's **black and dirty**?
—I'm sure I can think of something. Yes. There's **coal**, for example.

**1. brown and   mud
   dirty**

**2. white and   snow
   cold**

**3. white and   sugar
   sweet**

**4. yellow and   sunshine
   warm**

**5. green and   grass
   soft**

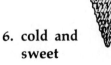

**6. cold and   ice cream
   sweet**

—Something must be wrong.
  Why isn't there any **beer**?
—There's a strike at the **brewery**.

—Something must be wrong.
  Why aren't there any **newspapers**?
—There's a strike at the **printer**.

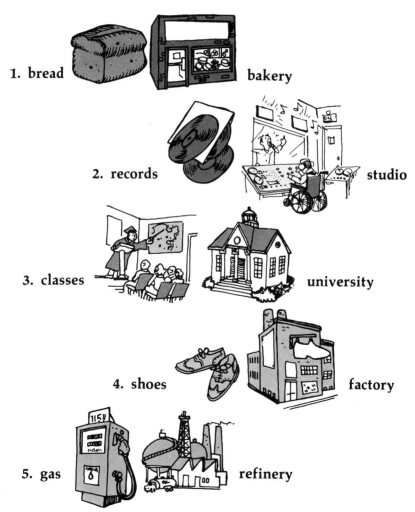

1. bread   bakery

2. records   studio

3. classes   university

4. shoes   factory

5. gas   refinery

Read & Predict

THE NIGHT SANTA GOT STUCK IN THE CHIMNEY

That year we spent Christmas with Uncle Percy, my father's rich brother. He lived in a big house in a lonely part of Vermont. We had started out early on Christmas Eve, but it was very late by the time we caught sight of Uncle Percy's house.   5

My wife and I and the three children climbed out of the car. Suddenly my little girl Jane shouted, "Look, Daddy and Mommy! I can see Santa Claus on the roof!"

We looked up to where Jane was pointing. Neither of us saw anything, of course. My wife and I smiled over our five-   10
year-old's head, and we all went inside. Soon we had put the children to bed and Uncle Percy had brought out all the toys he had bought for them. He couldn't wait to show us every-thing; the furniture and floor were covered with games, dolls, cars, trains and books. Then we heard a noise. It was Jane.   15

"Daddy, Daddy. I can hear Santa Claus on the roof!"

"Go back to bed, Jane, or Santa won't come."

Jane went back to bed, and we began wrapping Uncle Percy's presents. "Oh, Uncle Percy, all of these must have been terribly expensive," my wife said.   20

"Oh, the price isn't important. None of my relatives make me as happy as you do. Each of your children is special to me."

Just then I remembered I had forgotten to put the car in the garage. I went out. Just as I was closing the garage door, I heard a terrible scream. I rushed inside. Uncle Percy was   25
in front of the fireplace. Something was hanging from the chimney . . . no *somebody* was stuck in the chimney! We got him out and put him on the rug.

"Is he still breathing? He's not dead, is he?"

"No, just a little shocked. I think we have Jane's Santa   30
Claus," said Uncle Percy.

What did Percy mean? You'll find our explanation on page 35.

DO YOU REMEMBER?

1. In which state did Uncle Percy live?
2. How many people started out for his house?
3. What did Jane say she saw on the roof?
4. What had Uncle Percy bought for the children?
5. Describe what happened next.

Partner Practice

—I'm hungry. Do we have any **fruit**?

—Yes, I'm sure there's some.

—Where is it?

—I think it's in the refrigerator.

—I'm hungry. Do we have any **crackers**?

—Yes, I'm sure there are some.

—Where are they?

—I think they're in the cupboard.

 Use the pictures and names of other foods you know to make dialogues of your own.

MEMORY BANK

candy	eggs	cheese	cereal
cookies	sausage	oranges	bread
nuts	cake	pie	bananas

—The doctor told him he **ate too much.**
—Yes, anybody who **eats that much** had better be careful.

1. **smoked too much**
2. **drank too much**
3. **worried too much**
4. **worked too much**

5. **slept too little**
6. **exercised too little**
7. **ate too little**
8. **rested too little**

—Have you sold a lot of cars this year?

—No, I don't do much business now.

—Have you had a lot of parties lately?

—No, I don't do much entertaining now.

—Have you played a lot of tennis recently?

—No, I don't get much exercise now.

—Have you received a lot of letters this week?

—No, I don't get much mail now.

—Have you bought a lot of new records lately?

—No, I don't listen to much music now.

—Have you drunk a lot of wine this month?

—No, I don't drink much wine now.

—What's happened to you? Don't you enjoy life any more?

—No, not much.

HOW ABOUT YOU?

Work with your partner, asking and answering questions about things you've done a lot, too much, not much or too little, lately.

Read & Understand

12 Park Place
Medford, NY
May 4, 1991

Dear Karen,

Let me tell you it was such a shock to get your letter. You're the last person in the world I'd ever think would be in a three-car accident! Most of the people I know have had an accident at some time or another, but you're such a careful and considerate driver. None of your friends had heard about it until I told them.

Anyway, you're alive, and that's all that matters. What about your car? I hope you were well-insured, since it sounds like the damage was quite extensive. Will you try to have the car repaired or is it a total loss?

You remember Leon, don't you? He's in the used car business now. If you need another car, perhaps he can help you. He's got some really cheap ones on his lot.

Otherwise, I have no real news. Life is the same as always. Work is dull. The weather's wet and cold. I'll bet you're glad you got away from this place when you did. Must close now. Be happy and get well soon!

Love,
Gloria

DO YOU REMEMBER?

1. When was the letter written?
2. Who wrote the letter?
3. Who got the letter?
4. What had happened to Karen?
5. Why was Gloria surprised about Karen's accident?
6. In what way might Leon be able to help Karen?
7. Where do you think Gloria works?

Listen & Understand

THE ROBBERY

1. What had Sandra Marks been doing when the telephone rang?

a.
b.
c.

2. Where had the robbery taken place?

a.
b.
c.

3. How had the robber broken into the house?

a.
b.
c.

4. What had he stolen?

a.
b.
c.

5. What did Sandra find?

a.
b.
c.

6. How did Sandra know for certain who the robber was?

a.
b.
c.

Partner Practice

Look at the pictures and make the correct sentence for each.

1.   2.   3.

Each		boys		new.
Neither	of the	students	is	tall.
One		cars		eating.

1.   2.   3.

Each		men		waiting for a bus.
Neither	of the	women	was	feeling well.
One		children		eating an apple.

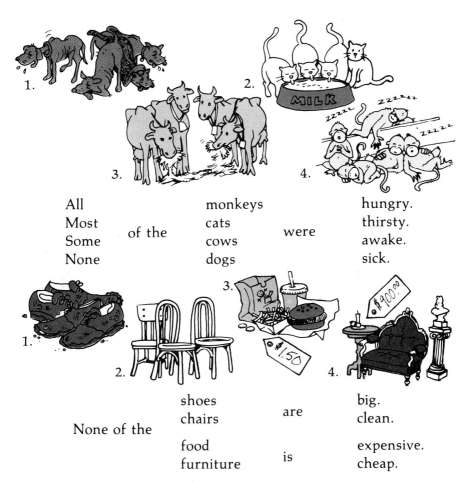

All		monkeys		hungry.
Most	of the	cats	were	thirsty.
Some		cows		awake.
None		dogs		sick.

		shoes	are	big.
None of the		chairs		clean.
		food	is	expensive.
		furniture		cheap.

1. Each of the men (have, has) a car.
2. None of the women (have, has) a cat.
3. All the children (was, were) playing in the street.
4. Neither of the boys (is, are) eating.
5. Most of these cars (is, are) fast.
6. Most of the bread (is, are) fresh.
7. Some of them (walk, walks) to school.
8. None of my friends (goes, go) by bus.
9. None of those women (has, have) husbands.
10. One of the boys (is, are) my brother.

Read & Predict

THE ACCIDENT

The car was obviously traveling too fast when it passed the truck on a curve. It skidded, collided with a telephone pole, and crashed into the waves of the Pacific Ocean below.

The truck driver was able to pull the two passengers—a man and a boy—from the car onto the beach. The police and an ambulance arrived quickly on the scene, but for the driver of the car, it was too late. The man was dead, and the boy unconscious. 5

The ambulance rushed the boy to the nearest hospital. There the police officers who were investigating the accident looked through the papers they had found in the dead man's car. "It looks like they were on their way to the airport. There are two tickets here for Flight 561 to Singapore. Mr. Paul Cavendish . . . and James Cavendish. Must have been father and son. The flight was at 7:15. They were probably afraid of arriving late. Some people never learn, do they? Better too late in this world than too early in the next." 10

15

A nurse came into the waiting room. "How's the boy, nurse?" "It's too early to tell. They'll have to operate. They've called in the best surgeon available."

In the operating room, the surgeon was ready. But the surgeon took one look at the boy and said, "I can't operate on this boy—he's my son!" 20

 How could this be? You'll find our explanation on page 40.

DO YOU REMEMBER?

1. Was the car speeding at the time of the accident?
2. Where did it try to pass a truck?
3. What happened next?
4. What did the truck driver do?
5. What happened to the passengers?
6. What did the police find in the dead man's car?
7. What was going to happen to the boy at the hospital?
8. What doctor was called in?
9. Was the man who had driven the car really the boy's father?

Partner Practice

—Do you think you'll get both of these **records**
for your birthday?
—Well, I hope that I'll get at least one of them!

—Would you like all of the **grapefruit**?
—No, but I'd like half of it, please.

MEMORY BANK		
1. magazines	2. pens	3. tapes
4. photos	5. books	6. brushes
1. newspaper	2. toast	3. coffee
4. milk	5. tea	6. butter

—Would you like a **glass of milk?**
—No, just **half a glass,** please.

1. a slice of bread   **2. a piece of cake**   **3. a cup of coffee**

—Do you know what he is
  going to write on?
—Yes, he said that he was going to
  buy a piece of paper.

1. Do you know what he is
   going to write with?

a piece of chalk

2. Do you know what she is
   going to paint with?

a can of paint

3. Do you know what she is
   going to wash it with?

a bar of soap

4. Do you know what they are
   going to light it with?

a book of matches

5. Do you know what they are
   going to cut it with?

a pair of scissors

6. Do you know what they are
   going to tie it with?

a ball of string

THE ACCIDENT
The surgeon was the boy's mother!

Read & Understand

THE LAND OF DREAMS

In the 1840's, California was almost uninhabited. There were a few Spanish missions, some ranchers and farmers, and of course, bandits who stole anything they could find.

In 1848, everything changed. Gold was discovered, and
5 people from all over the country rushed to California. They all dreamed of making their fortunes by finding gold. Mining towns were built anywhere gold was found. As a rule, these towns had no more than a saloon, a hotel, a stable, a jail—and a cemetery.

10   Almost a century later people again rushed to California. This time, they dreamed of making their fortunes not in gold, but in the movies. Los Angeles, a large city that was not even there in 1848, had become the movie capital of the world. These were the days of the great movie stars—actors and
15 actresses like Cary Grant and Rita Hayworth—heroes and heroines like John Wayne and Susan Hayward. Thousands of would-be stars dreamed of being a Hollywood prince or princess.

Few people look for gold now, and Los Angeles is no
20 longer a movie city. It's a factory town where time is money and TV companies control the time. The California scenery has changed, too. A century or so ago there were unclimbed, snow-topped mountains, uninhabited deserts, and unspoiled beaches with high surf. The scenery is still there, but so are
25 thousands of miles of highways, millions of cars, dozens of suburbs—and smog. Most films are now made inside, and the best place to find gold is in a jewelry store.

DO YOU REMEMBER?

1. Did California have many people in 1845?
2. What made people rush to California in 1848?
3. What were the mining towns like?
4. What city became the movie capital of the world?
5. What kind of city is Los Angeles today?
6. How did California's scenery look a century or more ago? How has the scenery changed?

Listen & Understand

THE MONEY HOLE

1. The story began in
   a. 1975   b. 1795   c. 1775

2. Daniel found the tree
   a. in a boat   b. in a hole   c. in an open space

3. They had gone down
   a. 100 feet   b. 10 feet   c. 20 feet

4. They discovered
   a. nothing   b. a box   c. logs

5. They had to give up because the hole was
   a. too deep   b. full of water   c. ninety feet deep

6. In 1849, he found a
   a. rock   b. tunnel to the sea   c. plug

7. The Oak Island Company gave up because they had no more
   a. drills   b. money   c. cement

8. They were killed by
   a. gas   b. the sea water   c. the new tunnel

9. They have spent
   a. $400,000   b. $40,000   c. $4,000,000

10. Which is true?
    a. There is no money in the hole.
    b. There is nothing in the hole.
    c. Nobody knows. The Money Hole is still a mystery.

Partner Practice

SYLLABLES AND STRESS

Words are made up of syllables. These are one-syllable words.

claim	brave	bill	nut	hot	bet
rain	plan	split	mud	stop	red

In words of two or more syllables, one of the syllables will be pronounced with more stress—more force—than the other(s). Notice that the stress changes from word to word.

1. sentence (**sen** tence)
2. witness (**wit** ness)
3. resent (re **sent**)
4. expect (ex **pect**)
5. innocent (**in** no cent)
6. newspaper (**news** pa per)
7. employment (em **ploy** ment)
8. confusion (con **fu** sion)

In words of three or more syllables, stress changes too.

1. intelligent (in **tel** li gent)
2. reliable (re **li** a ble)
3. duplication (du pli **ca** tion)
4. continuation (con tin u **a** tion)
5. university (u ni **ver** si ty)
6. inconsiderate (in con **sid** er ate)

Sentence stress is important, too. You can change the whole meaning of a sentence by changing the stressed word.

1. —Are *you* learning Spanish?
   —No, my *sister's* learning Spanish.

2. —Are you learning *Spanish?*
   —No, I'm learning *English.*

3. —Are you *learning* Spanish?
   —No, I'm *teaching* Spanish.

4. —Is *Jack's* sister learning Spanish?
   —No, *Peter's* sister is learning Spanish.

5. —Is Jack's *sister* learning Spanish?
   —No, Jack's *brother* is learning Spanish.

—Have you sold your
 house yet?
—No, it seems **difficult**
 to **sell.**

—Have you built that
 model yet?
—No, but it seems **easy**
 to **build.**

1. Has she found that report yet? (impossible)
2. Have you fixed your radio yet? (difficult)
3. Has he made his decision yet? (simple)
4. Have you read this story yet? (confusing)
5. Have you played this game yet? (exciting)

—What's the matter?
—There seems to be **a fly in my drink!**

1. hole in your sweater
2. gorilla in the garden
3. nail in my shoe

4. fire in the wastebasket
5. piece of gum on my chair
6. bee in your hair

—Where's the nearest **bank,** please?
—There's one just around the corner.

1.

2.

3.

4.

—Was the **concert** crowded?
—Yes, there were thousands of people there.

1.

2.

3.

4.

MEMORY BANK

| 1. post office | 2. restroom | 3. gas station | 4. parking lot |
| 1. theater | 2. park | 3. movie | 4. stadium |

Miracles

Why, who makes much of a miracle?
As to me I know of nothing else but miracles,
Whether I walk the streets of Manhattan,
Or dart my sight over the roofs of houses toward the sky,
Or wade with naked feet along the beach just in the edge of
   the water,
Or stand under the trees in the woods,
Or talk by day with any one I love, or sleep in the bed at
   night with any one I love,
Or sit at table at dinner with the rest,
Or look at strangers opposite me riding in the car,
Or watch honey-bees busy around the hive of a summer
   forenoon
Or animals feeding in the fields,
Or birds, or the wonderfulness of insects in the air,

Or the wonderfulness of the sundown, or of stars shining so
   quiet and bright,
Or the exquisite delicate thin curve of the new moon in spring;
These with the rest, one and all, are to me miracles,
The whole referring, yet each distinct and in its place.

To me every hour of the light and dark is a miracle,
Every cubic inch of space is a miracle,
Every square yard of the surface of the earth is spread with
   the same,
Every foot of the interior swarms with the same.
To me the sea is a continual miracle,
The fishes that swim — the rocks — the motion of the waves —
   the ships with men in them,
What stranger miracles are there?

Walt Whitman

Fast Track: *Read and Research*

FIGHTER FOR BORNEO'S HIDDEN PEOPLE

Harrison Ngau, a Kayan tribesman in Malaysian Borneo, has endured imprisonment, house arrest and government harassment for several years. His "crime:" helping Borneo's indigenous people try to halt the rampant logging that is destroying their way of life and some of the earth's most ancient tropical forests.

When timber interests first came to Ngau's area in the state of Sarawak in 1977, several thousand people lived entirely off the forests. But logging and settlement plans have reduced that number to fewer than 500 Penan tribespeople, who still cling to nomadic ways. Even these remaining nomadic clans are threatened by powerful trading companies, merchants and local politicians, who continue to push logging operations even deeper into the interior.

Ngau became concerned about logging in the late 1970s when its devastating effects began to become apparent. In 1982 he set up a branch of Friends of the Earth in Sarawak to help preserve the forests the Penans call "our bank and our shops." Ngau and his colleagues became investigators, exposing links between logging companies and politicians. Later, when the Penans found the courts stacked in favor of timber

MULTINATIONAL COMPANIES

Since timber interests first came to Borneo, life has changed drastically for the inhabitants of that part of the world. The article in this unit does not state whether these "interests" are national or multinational. Nowadays, it is sometimes difficult to know what is a national company.

interests, they took the desperate step of blockading logging roads. Ngau and Friends of the Earth provided legal help and made the Penans' plight the focus of international protests. "It is now time to look after our place so that it will have a future," says Ngau, who spent 60 days in prison for his efforts to help stop the logging.

In the face of indomitable tribespeople and pressure from foreign environmentalists, the Sarawak government has begun a dialogue with the Penans, and Malaysians have begun to respect those people who choose to live in the forests. Thanks to Ngau and his colleagues, there is a sliver of hope that the grim destruction of Sarawak may be halted.

Research Topics

1. List the 10 biggest companies in your country. (How you define "big" is up to you.)
2. Who are the owners or majority shareholders of the companies on your list?
3. Where is the head office of the parent company?
4. How many people does the company employ? Are they employed in your country or somewhere else?
5. What are the advantages and disadvantages of multinational ownership?

BORNEO

Harrison Ngau is a Kayan tribesman in Malaysian Borneo. What do you know about Borneo?

Research Topics

1. Where is Borneo?
2. What is the political status of Borneo? Is it an independent nation or does it belong to one or more other countries?
3. Is Borneo the accepted name of the country?
4. What sort of people live there? Are they all from the same tribe or racial background?
5. What multinational interests are there in the country?
6. What agriculture, industrial and manufactured goods does the country produce? What are its sources of energy?

WAY OF LIFE

The Penan tribespeople of Borneo have had their way of life changed for them. Fewer than 500 still cling to their nomadic existence. Have they changed their way of life willingly for a better future or have they been forced to adapt to a foreign and less attractive lifestyle?

Research Topics

1. Find out what you can about the Penan tribe of Borneo or some other tribe living in another part of the world.
2. How many people make up the tribe?
3. What is their way of life? (religion, family, economy, industry)
4. How is their way of life threatened from the outside?
5. How do they react to outside influence?
6. What sort of contact do they have with the rest of the world?
7. What does the future hold for them?

3

What do you think you'll be reading about in this unit?

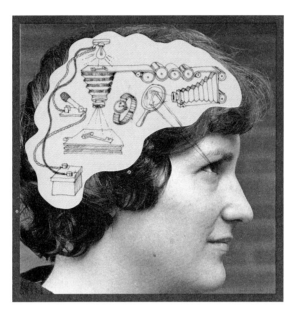

Partner Practice

—Which country will you visit if you win the lottery?
—I'll go to **Canada** or **Spain.**

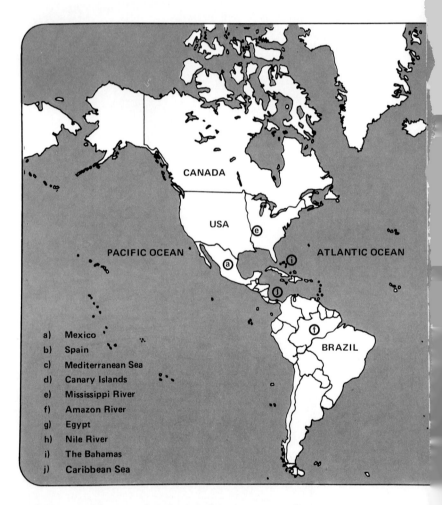

a)   Mexico
b)   Spain
c)   Mediterranean Sea
d)   Canary Islands
e)   Mississippi River
f)   Amazon River
g)   Egypt
h)   Nile River
i)   The Bahamas
j)   Caribbean Sea

—What would you do if you became a millionaire?
—I'd take a cruise in the **Mediterranean.**
—Where would you like to spend a few days?
—Either on **Rhodes** or **Sicily.**

—Where will Bill go on his vacation?

—He hopes he'll be able to go to the **Canary Islands.**

—The **Canary Islands**! They're in the **Atlantic Ocean,** aren't they?

—Yes, that's right.

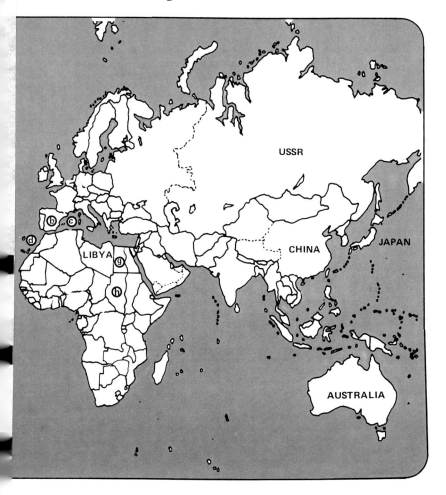

—I would go to **London** if I could afford it.

—Why would you like to be in **London**?

—Because it's so beautiful on the **Thames.**

Read & Predict

SMARTER THAN THE AVERAGE DOG

Ramon was very proud of his dog Blackie. Whenever he got the chance, he would ask his dog to entertain his friends with some tricks.

One day Ramon went to see his friend Frank. Frank had been sick at home with a bad cold for four days. "How do you feel?" asked Ramon. "Worse than yesterday," replied Frank. "I have a terrible cough, a fever, and there's no medicine in the house." 5

"Cheer up, Frank. I'll send Blackie to the local drugstore for a bottle of medicine. He'll be back before you know it." 10 Ramon put a five-dollar bill in Blackie's mouth and the dog ran down the street. "And keep the change," Ramon shouted after him. Ramon sat down and waited.

"Oh Ramon, don't be so silly. You know that dog won't be back with any medicine." "Oh yes he will," replied Ramon. 15 "You can bank on it." Half an hour later, however, Blackie had not returned. Ramon was feeling embarrassed, and resented his friend's little smile.

"Something has obviously happened to him," said Ramon. "He obeys me as a rule." "I think that five dollars is a total 20 loss. Time to face the music, Ramon," Frank laughed. Just then Frank saw Blackie coming down the street. He let Blackie in. Frank was shocked to see that the dog had the medicine.

"Good boy," said Ramon. "But what took you so long?" Blackie ran over to the window, barking and wagging his tail. 25 Ramon looked and saw a bone on the lawn.

Why had Blackie been delayed?
Our explanation is on page 57.

1. What would Ramon do whenever he got the chance?
2. What was wrong with Frank?
3. Where did Ramon send Blackie?
4. Why didn't Ramon think he would get any money back?
5. What did Frank say about the five dollars?
6. How did Frank feel when he saw Blackie with the medicine?
7. What did Blackie do at the window?

Partner Practice

—He's **an actor.**
—She's **an actress.**
—They **act on TV.**

1. **waiter   waitress**
   serve food in a restaurant

2. **host   hostess**
   give parties

3. **prince   princess**
   are members of royalty

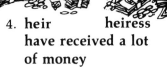

4. **heir   heiress**
   have received a lot
   of money

5. **hero   heroine**
   are big stars in the movies

1. This is the party's . . . , Susan Grant.
2. Rose is the best . . . in the restaurant.
3. Charles is the . . . of England.
4. Jane Goodie is the . . . of that movie.
5. She became an . . . when her uncle died.
6. My favorite . . . in the theater is Helen Home.
7. Find our . . . and tell him we want to order dinner now.

—Where is **money** kept?
—It's kept in a **bank**.

—Where are **bees** kept?
—They're kept in a **bee hive**.

1. clothes   closet

2. ice cream   freezer

3. sugar   sugar bowl

4. cows   barn

5. jewelry   wall safe

6. files   filing cabinet

7. fish   fish tank

8. photos   photo album

9. trash   trash can

10. cookies   cookie jar

Read & Understand

JOHN HENRY

John Henry is one of the famous heroes of American folklore. He worked on the Chesapeake and Ohio Railroad toward the end of the nineteenth century.

John Henry was very strong. He made his mark in history
5 because he could work harder and faster than any other man on the railroad. Curious people came from far and wide to see him hammer steel spikes through the hard earth.

When the Big Bend Tunnel was started, trouble began. The mountain seemed impossible to get through. The men
10 who were building the railroad bought a new invention, a drilling machine, to try to speed up the tunneling. The other railroad workers welcomed the machine, but not John Henry. He stubbornly insisted he could work harder and faster than any machine. "I'll die with a hammer in my hand, before I
15 let a machine make a fool out of me," he said.

And so a competition was planned. It would last for 45 minutes, or until one of the competitors gave up. The winner would be the man or machine who had drilled farthest into the rock. Hundreds of people went to Big Bend to watch this
20 great attraction.

After 30 minutes, the machine broke down, but John Henry kept right on working for 45 minutes. The machine had drilled only nine feet. John Henry, 15 feet. He had won a great victory, but the effort had been too much. As the song
25 goes, "He died with the hammer in his hand, Lord, Lord . . . died with the hammer in his hand."

DO YOU REMEMBER?

1. On what project did John Henry work?
2. Why did he become famous?
3. Why was a drilling machine bought?
4. How did John Henry feel about the machine?
5. What were the rules of the competition?
6. By how much did John Henry do better than the machine?
7. How did John Henry die?

Listen & Understand

1. What did he have for lunch?

a.

b.

c.

2. What doesn't he have?

a.

b.

c.

3. What's the matter with him?

a.

b.

c.

4. How much does he make an hour?

a.

b.

c.

5. What were they playing?

a.

b.

c.

SMARTER THAN THE AVERAGE DOG
Blackie had stopped to buy himself a bone with the change.

Partner Practice

—What was the matter with him?
Didn't he feel well?
—No, he said he had **a cold.**

1. a cough

2. a headache

3. a fever

4. a broken ankle

5. an upset stomach

6. a sore throat

—How much does a **delivery boy** earn?
—About **two dollars an hour,** I'd guess.

1. secretary	$100/day
2. lawyer	$1000/week
3. pilot	$3500/month
4. dentist	$50,000/year
5. rock group	$350,000/show

—What's the temperature going to be like today?
—It's going to be **hot—at least 90** degrees.

1. cold/only 10　　**2. mild/about 60**　　**3. chilly/about 40**

—How far is it to **New York**?
—It's **99** miles.

TO NEW YORK 99

Washington 100　　**Santiago 999**　　**Montreal 1100**

1.　　2.　　3.

—How heavy is that **box**?
—It's **15 pounds.**

1. 3 tons　　**2. 8 ounces**　　**3. 30 pounds**

—How long is that **scarf**?
—It's **2 feet!**

1. 2 inches　　**2. 5 yards**　　**3. 6 feet**

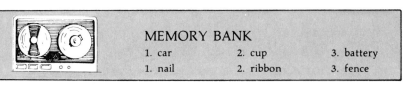

MEMORY BANK

1. car	2. cup	3. battery
1. nail	2. ribbon	3. fence

Read & Predict

THE ABSENT-MINDED PROFESSOR

I once knew a man whose memory was very bad. Richard Rudd was so forgetful that he would sometimes forget what he was talking about in the middle of a sentence. As a rule, his wife had to remind him about his appointments, his classes—even his meals. Since Rudd was a professor at a well-known university, his forgetfulness was often an embarrassment, and he didn't hit it off with some of the other professors. It wasn't that he was unintelligent, as some critical people tended to believe. He was just very, very absent-minded. 5

One hot summer's day, Professor Rudd decided to take his children to the beach. The seaside town he planned to visit was about a three-hour train ride away. To make the trip more interesting for his young children, he kept the name of the town a secret. Unfortunately, by the time Rudd had arrived at the train station, the poor forgetful man had forgotten the name of his destination himself. Fortunately, a friend of his happened to be in the station. He offered to take care of the children while Rudd went back home to find out where he was going. 10

15

The professor's wife was surprised to see him again so soon, but she was amused when she heard what was the matter. She distrusted his memory, so she wrote the name of the town on a piece of paper. Satisfied that she had solved the problem, she sent her husband off again. Ten minutes later she was surprised to see him outside the house again. What was the matter now? 20

25

 You'll find our explanation on page 63.

DO YOU REMEMBER?
1. What kinds of things did Richard Rudd forget?
2. Why was his bad memory sometimes embarrassing?
3. What did some critical people say about Rudd?
4. Where did the professor decide to take his children?
5. How far away was the destination?
6. What happened at the train station?
7. Why did Rudd go home? What did his wife do? Why?
8. What happened ten minutes later?

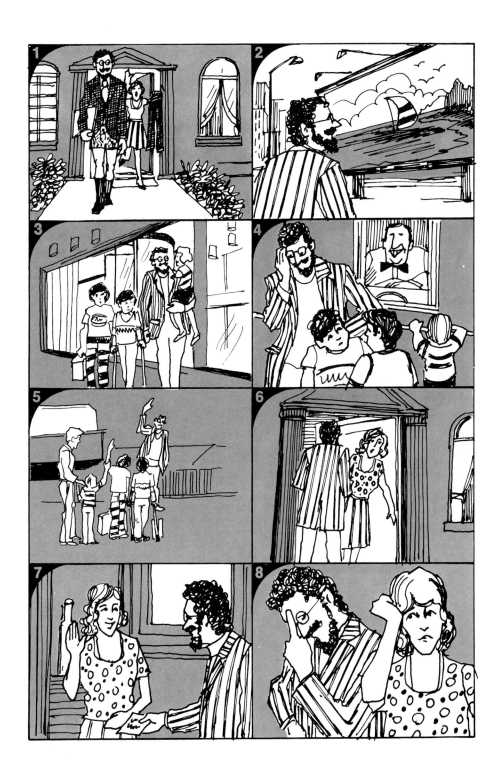

Partner Practice

—These are **clothes for women.**
—Are you sure?
—Yes, they are **women's clothes.**

1. toys for children

2. shoes for men

3. hats for policewomen

4. boots for fishermen

—This is a **shop for ladies.**
—Really?
—Yes, it's a **ladies' shop.**

1. school for girls

2. bike for boys

3. disco for teenagers

4. parking place for visitors

—Did you say **the trip** would be **a day** long?
—Yes. It will be **a day's** trip.

1. **your vacation**   **a week**
2. **the interview**   **a day**
3. **the flight**   **an hour**
4. **the wait**   **a month**

—Did **the Christmas holiday** last for **two days?**
—Yes, it was **a two-day holiday.**

1. Did the race last for thirty minutes?
2. Did the dinner last for two hours?
3. Did his cough last for a month?
4. Did the strike last for five days?
5. Did his surgery last for two hours?

—What's the **watch** made of?
—**Gold.**
—Are you sure it's made of **gold?**
—Yes, you can bank on it. It's a fine **gold watch.**

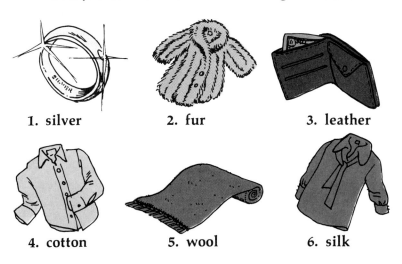

1. silver   2. fur   3. leather

4. cotton   5. wool   6. silk

THE ABSENT-MINDED PROFESSOR
The professor had forgotten where he had left his children!

Read & Understand

DON'T FORGET TO REMEMBER!

Read the following sets of numbers. It shouldn't take you more than about ten seconds.

876   935   290   143   841   986   405

Believe it or not, there are people who can
5 read these numbers as quick as a flash and
remember them for the rest of their lives. They
have "photographic" memories that can see
something and store it in their minds forever—
like a camera captures something forever on
10 film. Scientists think that about one person in
5,000 has this remarkable power to remember.

A 23-year-old American university student
made her mark by being able to read poems in
foreign languages she had never studied. She
15 could also recite the poems later without any
help. She explained that she could "see" the
pages in her mind. To prove this, she could even
say the poems backwards.

After months of experiments with the girl,
20 two scientists prepared a special test. They made
a huge "chessboard" with *10,000* black and
white squares put down in a haphazard fashion.
The girl studied the giant board for only a few
minutes. Months later, she could still describe
25 the position of all the squares perfectly!

DO YOU REMEMBER?

1. What's so special about "photographic" memories?
2. About how many people have such memories?
3. How did the student make her mark?
4. How did she prove that she could "see" the poems?
5. How were the chessboard squares put down?
6. How long did the girl study the board?
7. What could she do months later?

Listen & Understand

THE DAY WE LEFT HOME

1. When were their parents coming back?

a. b. c.

2. What did John want to fix?

a. b. c.

3. What crawled across the sink?

a. b. c.

4. What did they decide to cut?

a. b. c.

5. What did John break?

a. b. c.

6. Where were the rubber gloves?

a. b. c.

Partner Practice

—**Did you see the church on the side of the road?**
—**Yes, I saw it on the road-side.**

1. Did you find the boat on the bank of the river?
2. Did you eat lunch on the side of the mountain?
3. Did you photograph the scenery from the top of the hill?
4. Did you discover that gold on the floor of the ocean?

—What have you painted so far?
—I've painted the **door of the garage.**

1. roof of the house

2. legs of the table

3. arms of the chair

4. gate of the fence

5. windows of the house

6. doors of the truck

Sometimes we use special expressions to describe people or things.

1. as fat as a pig

2. as quick as a flash

3. as wise as an owl

4. as blind as a bat

5. as gentle as a lamb

6. as stubborn as a mule

7. as white as a ghost

8. as black as coal

9. as cold as ice

Use some of the expressions above to complete these sentences.

1. —I'm just freezing.
   —So am I. My feet are . . . .
2. —Can you see without your glasses?
   —No, I'm . . . .
3. —Mary gets things done fast, as a rule.
   —Yes, she's . . . .
4. —Bill doesn't seem to hit it off with many people.
   —That's because he's . . . .
5. —Who's the most intelligent person you know?
   —My grandfather. He made his mark in business. He's . . . .
6. —I can't see anything, can you?
   —No, it's . . . in this tunnel.

ON YOUR OWN

Work with a partner. Describe people you know with these expressions. Do you know any others like these? You can write some of your sentences for extra credit.

The Unknown Citizen

(to JS/07/M378 This Marble Monument is Erected by the State)

He was found by the Bureau of Statistics to be
One against whom there was no official complaint,
And all reports on his conduct agree
That, in the modern sense of an old-fashioned word, he was a
   saint,
For in everything he did he served the Greater Community.

Except for the War till the day he retired
He worked in a factory and never got fired,
But satisfied his employers, Fudge Motors Inc.
Yet he wasn't a scab or odd in his views,
For his Union reports that he paid his dues,
(Our report on his Union shows it was sound)
And our Social Psychology workers found
That he was popular with his mates and liked a drink.
The Press are convinced that he bought a paper every day
And that his reactions to advertisements were normal in every
    way
Policies taken out in his name prove that he was fully insured,
And his Health-card shows he was once in hospital but left it
    cured.
Both Producers Research and High-Grade Living declare
He was fully sensible to the advantages of the Instalment Plan
And had everything necessary to the Modern Man,
A phonograph, a radio, a car and a frigidaire.
Our researchers into Public Opinion are content
That he held the proper opinions for the time of year;
When there was peace, he was for peace; when there was war,
    he went.
He was married and added five children to the population,
Which our Eugenist says was the right number for a parent of
    his generation,
And our teachers report that he never interfered with their
    education.
Was he free? Was he happy? The question is absurd:
Had anything been wrong, we should certainly have heard.

W.H. Auden

LOVE CANAL'S FEISTY MUCKRAKER

She was a storybook Niagara Falls, New York housewife, baking bread, keeping a spotless kitchen and raising her family in the neighborhood known locally as Love Canal. But in 1978 Lois Gibbs' life took an abrupt turn. That was when she became convinced that the toxic-goo seeping from an abandoned chemical-waste dump three blocks from her home was making her children — and those of her neighbor — sick.

Stymied by stonewalling corporate and government bureaucrats, Gibbs summoned talents she did not know she had. Over a period of two years, she knocked on doors, passed out petitions, gave speeches, picketed, sat in, got arrested and, finally, took hostage a couple of Environmental Protection Agency officials until the FBI ordered her to release them. That got President Carter's attention and ultimately forced the Government to evacuate the neighborhood.

The woman who transformed Love Canal into an international symbol of the dangers of toxic waste has become a role model for a generation of homemaking "ecocrusaders." With part of the $30,000 that New York State paid for her home, she packed her children and her belongings into a trailer and headed for Washington and a career as a professional lobbyist. Today she runs the Citizens' Clearinghouse for Hazardous Wastes, a consulting service based in Arlington, Virginia, for communities in Love Canal-like situations.

"The only way to make change is to do it on the local level and move up," says Gibbs. Two of her biggest battles have been protecting 250 members of the mining community of Kellogg, Idaho, where lead has been leaching from an old Gulf Resources smelter, and trying to help 400 families living near five toxic lagoons at the Mill Service dump site in Yukon, Pennsylvania.

INDUSTRIAL POLLUTION

Lois Gibbs and her family were threatened by toxic waste from a factory that was no longer operating. In addition to pollution from existing industries, our lives are constantly threatened by the remnants of industries that existed before we became aware of many of the problems that stem from industrial waste.

Research Topics

1. Chart the main areas of industrial activity in your country or local area.
2. Catalogue the waste products that these industries produce.
3. List the effects these waste products may have on our health and environment.
4. Investigate efforts made to limit the effects of this waste.
5. Consider the benefits these industries bring to the community.
6. Decide whether the negative effects of the industries investigated balance or outweigh the positive effects.

MAKING YOUR VOICE HEARD

Lois Gibbs was a determined woman. She was probably called many less flattering names by those who opposed her.

Government and corporate bureaucrats blocked her at every turn, but she persisted. Is there a limit to how far a person or group may go to make their voices heard or gain their ends? Does the end justify the means?

Research Topics

1. Consider a "cause." It may be political, ecological, social, emotional—whatever.
2. Describe the aims of the cause.
3. Describe the opposition to the cause.
4. Describe the means used so far to get results.
5. Report on the actions of those opposed to the cause.
6. What extreme actions could be used? Justify these actions.

TRADITIONAL ROLES

Lois Gibbs was a storybook housewife: baking bread, keeping a spotless kitchen and raising her family in the neighborhood known as Love Canal. She gave all this up and became the role model for homemaking "ecocrusaders."

What are our storybook roles? How are we influenced by our parents and those around us?

Research Topics

1. List the different household chores in your home.
2. Determine who does what on a regular basis. How many chores are shared?
3. Who works outside the home? How are decisions concerning purchases, investments, holidays, etc., reached?
4. Is there any pattern in spare time activities?
5. What makes a "good" mother, father, son or daughter?
6. Are we all the same or are we different? Should we try to eradicate or encourage any role differences between the sexes?

What do you think you'll be reading about
in this unit?

Partner Practice

—Didn't **they** say anything?
—No, **they** just shook **their** heads.

—Didn't **she** say anything?
—No, **she** just shrugged **her** shoulders.

 Now make up more questions and answers of your own. Use *he, she, we, you* and *they* as you practice.

—Is this **your** book?
—No, **my** book is over there.
—Oh, is **yours** the one on **photography?**
—Yes, that's **mine.**

MEMORY BANK		
I	my	mine
he	his	his
she	her	hers
we	our	ours
you	your	yours
they	their	theirs

Partner Practice

—Do you have **Ralph's racquet**?
—Yes, I've brought his **racquet** with me.

1. **your sister's**

2. **your brother's**

3. **your parents'**

4. **my**

5. **our**

6. **your**

—I haven't seen **Bob** for a long time.
—Neither have I. I wonder what's happened to him.
—I don't really care. We don't hit it off, anyway.

1. **Elinor**   2. **Kathy**
3. **Ted and Jack**   4. **Sally and Jane**
5. **Karen**   6. **Gail and Max**

—I didn't know he was one of **your daughter's** friends.
—Oh, he's been a friend of **hers** for years.

1. **your father's**   2. **your parents'**
3. **your**   4. **your family's**
5. **your sister's**   6. **your son's**

Read & Predict

UNLUCKY IN LOVE

During the war, a pilot was shot down over enemy territory. Fortunately, he was saved from his burning plane by a group of nuns from a nearby convent. He was knocked unconscious during the crash landing, and when he came to, he was astonished to find a woman leaning over him.   5

It was Sister Maria, the nun in charge. She said to the pilot, "This convent is a teaching hospital. We have many young girls here, learning how to be nurses. We will hide you here as long as possible, but you will have to obey very strict rules." The pilot promised to obey the rules. "I'll do what you   10
say. You can bank on it," he said.

The pilot agreed to disguise himself as a nurse. He was not allowed to talk with either the nuns or the nurses. He had to stay in his small room as much as possible. By shaving twice a day, wearing a wig and a nurse's uniform, he was able   15
to fool anybody at a distance. It was a difficult life, however. He felt very lonely, especially when one of the students caught his eye. She was very quiet and shy, and turned her head whenever she saw him looking her way. The pilot fell in love with her, and thought of her constantly. But he never tried   20
to speak to her.

One day, however, the pilot could stand it no longer, and broke his promise. He found the nurse working in the kitchen. He crossed over to her and said, "Please don't turn away. I've fallen in love with you." He started to put his arms   25
around the nurse, and then stepped back in amazement.

 What was his problem? Why was the pilot unlucky in love? You'll find our explanation on page 78.

DO YOU REMEMBER?

1. Where was the pilot shot down?
2. Who saved him?
3. What happened to the pilot during the landing?
4. What did Sister Maria tell the pilot?
5. What did the pilot agree to do?
6. What was his life like?
7. How did the pilot break his promise?

Partner Practice

IDIOMS

Sometimes the way a familiar word is used with other words makes an expression that has a special meaning. For example, you know the word *song*. If somebody says "I bought my car for a song," however, *song* now has a different meaning. *For a song* means *cheaply, for very little money*.

Here are some other expressions. See if you can guess what they mean; your teacher can help with any you can't figure out.

1. *hit it off* - I don't always hit it off with John.
   We don't agree on many things.

2. *face the music* - It's time to face the music.
   You have to tell Mary you broke her radio.

3. *as a rule* - I'm not here on Thursdays as a rule.
   I'm usually at home.

4. *make a mark* - He's really made his mark on the boss.
   She gave him a day off!

5. *bank on it* - I'll be there. You can bank on it.
   I wouldn't miss your party.

6. *a pretty penny* - Her new car cost a pretty penny.
   I wish I could afford one like that.

ON YOUR OWN

   Work with a partner and make sentences of your own with the expressions. Perhaps you know others you can share with the class.

> UNLUCKY IN LOVE
> The shy nurse was another pilot in disguise!

Some words in English sound the same, but have different meanings and spellings. Read these sentences.

1. —I like that *scent.* Is it a   —Yes, Bob *sent* it to me.
   new perfume?
2. —Who *made* the beds?   —The hotel *maid* did.
3. —Did you throw that ball   —No, I didn't. My brother
   through my window?   *threw* it.
4. —Did you tie this *knot?*   —No, I did *not.*
5. —You *knew* Dick's old   —Yes, I did. Don't tell me
   girl friend, didn't you?   he's got a *new* one.
6. —How did you *break* your   —The *brake* on my bike was
   arm?   broken.
7. —Where did you *meet* Jane?   —At the *meat* department.
8. —Why do you *sew?*   —*So* I can have a lot of clothes.
9. —Did you pick up *our* car?   —Yes, an *hour* ago.
10. —What can you *see?*   —The *sea*coast.
11. —I'm going *to* Sue's party.   —I am *too*—at *two* o'clock.

ON YOUR OWN

Work with a partner, and use some of the words from above to complete these sentences. Can you make sentences of your own as well?

1. Can you . . . this button on my shirt?
2. You . . . that our house burned down, didn't you?
3. Ask the . . . to vacuum the rugs today.
4. This window is so dirty I can't see . . . it.
5. . . . me at the restaurant at twelve-thirty.
6. Which do you like better, . . . or fish?
7. He left home an . . . ago.
8. Please help me tie a . . . in this string.
9. He . . . the ball to Tom.
10. Have you . . . that package to Julio yet?
11. Did you go . . . the movies last night?
12. I just . . . a great banana cake.

Read & Understand

LEFT . . . RIGHT . . . LEFT . . .

Since the beginning of time, some people (the right-handed ones) have believed that there is something wrong with left-handers. Left-handed people have been distrusted, or thought strange. If
5 you are left-handed, there's no need to feel lonely. Roughly a third of the world's population is left-handed, and unfair attitudes against "lefties" are gradually changing. Most parents no longer force children to use their right hands even though they
10 really prefer to use their left.

The right-handers of the world have begun to realize how unfair the world has been to its left-handed members. For a left-hander, scissors won't cut; can-openers won't work; cars with gear shifts
15 are difficult to drive. But at last, help is on the way for the "lefties." *Anything Left-handed* is a new shop in London. It offers, at reasonable prices, especially designed, reliable products for left-handed people. This shop has made its mark with everything from
20 left-handed scissors to toe nail clippers, potato peelers, pens, and golf clubs. The owner of *Anything Left-handed*, by the way, is right-handed.

 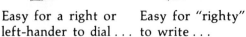 

Easy for a right or   Easy for "righty"   Almost impossible
left-hander to dial . . .   to write . . .   for poor "Lefty"

DO YOU REMEMBER?

1. How have left-handers been treated in the past?
2. About how many people in the world are left-handed?
3. What sorts of problems do left-handed people have?
4. What kind of store has opened in London?
5. Are the products in the store expensive?
6. What do you know about the shop's owner?

Listen & Understand

MY DAD

1. Which man is her dad?

a.

b.

c.

2. When is he very impatient?

a.

b.

c.

3. Where does he work?

a.

b.

c.

4. What unkind thing does he do?

a.

b.

c.

5. What does she want to be?

a.

b.

c.

Partner Practice

—Are the **scissors** sharp or dull?
—They're **dull**.

—Is the **music** loud or soft?
—It's **loud!**

1. old or new

2. expensive or cheap

3. warm or cold

4. dirty or clean

5. broken or fixed

6. big or small

7. fresh or stale

8. pretty or ugly

MEMORY BANK

1. jeans	2. gas	3. wine	4. clothes
5. stairs	6. glasses	7. bread	8. jewelry

—Can I have some more **cheese?**

—Yes, but there isn't much left.

—Can I have some more **potatoes?**

—Yes, but there aren't many left.

1. 2. 3.

4. 5. 6.

—Did you find some **bread?**

—Yes, but there was only a little left.

—Did you find some **eggs?**

—Yes, but there were only a few left.

1. 2. 3.

4. 5. 6.

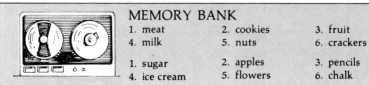

MEMORY BANK

1. meat	2. cookies	3. fruit
4. milk	5. nuts	6. crackers
1. sugar	2. apples	3. pencils
4. ice cream	5. flowers	6. chalk

Read & Predict

THE PERFECT PEARL

An elegant man entered a famous jewelry shop one day.
He said that he wanted to buy a pearl for his wife's birthday.
The price didn't matter, since business had been particularly
good for him that year. After examining a number of pearls,
he chose an exquisite black one that cost $5,000. He paid for   5
the gem in cash, shook hands with the jeweler, and left.

A few days later, the man returned and said that his wife
had liked the pearl so much that she wanted another one just
like it. It had to be exactly the same size and quality, as she
wanted a pair of earrings made. "Can you tell me how to get   10
hold of such a pearl?" asked the man. The jeweler replied, "I
would say it's impossible to find an exact duplicate of that
pearl. And if we could, it would cost you a pretty penny."

The millionaire insisted that the jeweler advertise in the
newspaper and offered $25,000 for the matching pearl. Many   15
people answered the ad, but nobody had a pearl that was
just right. Just when the jeweler had given up hope, a little
old lady came into his store. To his amazement, she pulled
the perfect pearl from her bag. "I don't like to part with it,"
she said. "I inherited it from my mother, and my mother   20
inherited it from hers. But I really need the money."

The jeweler was quick to pay the old lady before she
changed her mind. Then he called the millionaire's hotel.
The millionaire, however, could not be found.

Why? You'll find our explanation on page 88.

DO YOU REMEMBER?
1. Why did he want to buy a pearl?
2. Did he buy the first pearl he looked at?
3. Did he pay with his credit card?
4. Why did he return to the shop?
5. Why did the second pearl have to be a duplicate of
   the first?
6. How did the jeweler feel about finding a matching pearl?
7. How did he try to find it?
8. Where did he get the duplicate from?
9. Where did the old lady say the pearl had come from?

Partner Practice

IDIOMS

Here are some idiomatic uses of a familiar verb—**make.**
Discuss each, and then use in the sentences below.

make good	be successful	He made good as an engineer.
make off with	steal	He made off with all the jewels.
make out	see; under- stand	I can't make out what the sign says.
make up	be friends again	Let's make up and not fight any more.
make up for	give or do in place of	I hope these flowers will make up for my bad manners yesterday.

1. —Where in the world are we?
   —I don't know. I can't . . . what the map says.

2. —Are you still angry?
   —No. Let's . . . and be friends again.

3. —You're late again, Smith.
   —I know, sir. I'll . . . the lost time.

4. —What do you want to do for a living?
   —I want to . . . as a surgeon.

5. —Give me a list of what was stolen.
   —They . . . over $10,000 in diamonds and furs.

ON YOUR OWN

Work with a partner. Make incomplete sentences of
your own on paper. Then exchange papers with
another pair and complete their sentences.

Now you're going to work with idiomatic uses of **do.** Discuss as usual, and complete the sentences below.

do away with	kill	They should do away with that dog.
do	be okay/good	This hat will do.
do out of	take away; steal	He did me out of ten dollars!
do without	not have	I can't do without your help.
do up	wrap	Can you do up this package for me?

1. —Do you really care about me?
   —I *love* you! I can't . . . you!

2. —How did you like your first motorcycle ride?
   —To tell you the truth, I can . . . the motorcycle riding.

3. —Madam, I've shown you ten pairs of shoes.
   —I know, but none of them will . . . .

4. —Do you have Betty's present?
   —Yes, I'm going to . . . it . . . in pretty paper.

5. —The Baxter's dog is dangerous.
   —I know. I think they should . . . him.

6. —Why don't you and Tom hit it off?
   —He tried to . . . me . . . . . . the money I lent him.

ON YOUR OWN

Work with your partner. Make lists of things (or people) you would like to do away with or do without! What are some things you don't want to do without?

Read & Understand

THE JONKER DIAMOND

Jacobus Jonker was a diamond prospector in South Africa. He never really had much luck, and the longer he prospected, the less he believed in ever making his fortune. Imagine his feelings, then, when he found one of the biggest diamonds
5 in the world—right in his own back yard! There had been a heavy rainstorm, and the rains had washed away part of a hillside behind his house. And in the middle of the mud sat a huge diamond.

Jonker sold the stone to a diamond dealer for a pretty
10 penny—over three hundred thousand dollars! In New York, the diamond was resold—this time for almost eight hundred thousand dollars!

The true value of a diamond is never known until it has been cut. Once cut successfully, its value can increase a
15 thousand times. It's easy to understand why the owner of the Jonker diamond went to the best diamond cutter he knew. Kaplan, the cutter, studied the diamond for twelve whole months. When he felt he was ready to start work, he discovered a flaw. He had to begin his calculations all over
20 again—otherwise he might have destroyed the stone. Kaplan continued to study the stone; six more months passed. Finally, Kaplan said to the owner, "I'm ready to start my work. There will be one exquisite diamond that will be comparable to any in the world, and eleven small diamonds of first-class quality.
25 You can bank on it."

Kaplan waited a few more days until he felt he was in the best physical and mental condition possible. One mistake could lead to the total destruction of the stone. He picked up his tools and held his breath as he made the first blow. The
30 diamond split exactly as he had promised.

THE PERFECT PEARL
The "millionaire" and the old lady were thieves who worked together. The "duplicate" pearl that she sold to the jeweler was the same one the "millionaire" had bought.

Listen & Understand

MY FRIENDS

1. Elizabeth is
a. famous
b. boring
c. intelligent

2. Tom is
a. amusing
b. efficient
c. resentful

3. Henry is
a. confusing
b. careful
c. dangerous

4. Sara is
a. lovely
b. efficient
c. lonely

5. Peter is
a. enthusiastic
b. confusing
c. suspicious

6. Jane is
a. considerate
b. exciting
c. boring

Partner Practice

Ray and Charles had a big baseball game. They had asked their friends and families to play on their team. The game wasn't very successful, however. Before long, every player had hurt himself or herself in one way or another. Ray and Charles have lost the game, and are talking about their team members.

—Did Mary hurt herself?

—Yes, she hurt her leg.

—Did your father hurt himself?

—Yes, he hurt his hand.

—Did your brother hurt himself?

—Yes, he hurt his arm.

—Did your sister hurt herself?

—Yes, she hurt her finger.

—Did the twins hurt themselves?

—Yes, they hurt their heads.

—Did you hurt yourself?

—Yes, I hurt my foot. Did you hurt yourself?

—Yes, I hurt my back.

—So we both hurt ourselves, too. We'll all remember this game for a long time.

—Please—don't remind me. I'm already trying to forget it.

WORD BUILDING

If you add -ful to certain verbs and nouns, they become adjectives. The word hateful means "filled with hate"; careful means "filled with care." Discuss the words below, and then use them to complete the sentences.

hate	hateful	truth	truthful
care	careful	power	powerful
resent	resentful	wonder	wonderful
distrust	distrustful	thought	thoughtful
thank	thankful	hope	hopeful
help	helpful	pain	painful
forget	forgetful	beauty	beautiful

1. —Is your broken leg . . . ?
   —Of course. The . . . is terrible!
   —Well, I . . . you feel better soon.

2. —I . . . Jack. He doesn't always tell the truth.
   —I know. He should try to be more . . . .

3. —You're too generous. This watch
     must have cost a pretty penny.
   —Oh, don't . . . me. It was nothing.

4. —Is his new wife pretty?
   —More than pretty—. . . .

5. —Did you buy my ticket?
   —Oh, sorry. I've been so . . . lately.
   —How could you . . . ?
   —Well, my memory isn't very . . . .

6. —I . . . to tell you this, but I have to face the music.
   —What have you done wrong?
   —I broke this dish.
   —Don't worry. I bought it for a song.
     Just be more . . . next time.

ON YOUR OWN

Work with a partner and make sentences of your own.
You can write your sentences for extra credit.

The Sound of Silence

Hello darkness my old friend,
I've come to talk with you again,
Because a vision softly creeping,
Left its seeds while I was sleeping
And the vision that was planted in my brain
Still remains within the sound of silence.

In restless dreams I walked alone,
Narrow streets of cobblestone
'Neath the halo of a street lamp,
I turned my collar to the cold and damp
When my eyes were stabbed by the flash of a neon light
That split the night, and touched the sound of silence.

And in the naked light I saw
Ten thousand people maybe more,
People talking without speaking,
People hearing without listening,
People writing songs that voices never share
And no one dares disturb the sound of silence.

"Fools!" said I, "You do not know
Silence like a cancer grows.
Hear my words that I might teach you
Take my arms that I might reach you."
But my words like silent raindrops fell
And echoed, in the wells of silence.

And the people bowed and prayed
To the neon God they made,
And the sign flashed out its warning
In the words that it was forming.
And the sign said:
    "The words of the prophets are written
      on the subway walls and tenement halls"
And whispered in the sounds of silence.

Paul Simon

Fast Track: *Read and Research*

WALKS ON THE WILD SIDE

A long-distance walk for a worthy cause is hardly a new idea, but Michael Werikhe has taken the concept to new lengths. Over the past eight years, Werikhe, 33, has trekked thousands of miles across Africa and Europe to raise money to save the black rhino, one of the world's most endangered species.

Elephant tusks, rhino horns and leopard skins confiscated from poachers were a common sight in the "ivory room" of the Kenyan Game Department's Mombasa office, where Werikhe used to work. But a pair of 110 pound (50 kilograms) tusks brought in one day by a game warden induced him to start his one-man crusade. "Being an African, I see wildlife as part of my heritage," Werikhe says. "If wildlife goes, then part of me is dead. I wanted to campaign for wildlife in my own private way."

On his first wildlife walk, in 1982, Werikhe traveled 1,500 miles (2,400 kilometers), from Kampala, Uganda, through Kenya to Dar es Salaam, Tanzania, and back to Mombasa, with only a pet python named Survival for company. Lecturing to villagers and school-children, he raised about $30,000 for conservation groups. In 1988 Werikhe went to Europe, covering 1,800 miles (2,900 kilometers) in 135 days, and collected almost $1 million for rhino sanctuaries. Partly as a result of Werikhe's ef-forts, Kenya's black rhino population — once as low as 400 animals — has been slowly in-creasing since 1988. When Wer-ikhe is not on one of his journeys, he works as a superintendent of security at an auto plant. He plans to walk across the U.S. and hopes to eventually visit the Far East, where most rhino horn and elephant ivory are sold.

AFRICA

Several towns and countries in Africa are mentioned in this article (e.g., Mombasa, Kampala, Uganda and Kenya). The history of Africa is, in many ways, the history of colonialism.

Research Topics

1. Examine a political map of Africa and look at the various colonies.
2. Which nations colonized Africa?
3. How was Africa divided geographically into areas of influence?
4. What consequences did this division have for the development of various nations? Consider the laws, trade, language, social systems, etc.
5. What, if anything, is left of the old colonial system?

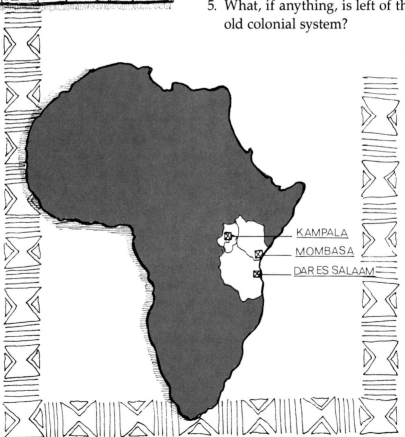

KAMPALA
MOMBASA
DAR ES SALAAM

WILDLIFE

Several endangered species are mentioned in the text, e.g. elephants, leopards and rhinos. Consider one of these animals — or any other endangered animal of your choice — and answer the following questions.

Research Topics

1. What is the animal's natural habitat? Why?
2. What are the natural enemies of the animal?
3. How have we endangered the animal?
4. How has the number of animals changed in the past century?
5. Why should this particular animal be protected?

CAMPAIGNS

Michael Werikhe is conducting a one-man campaign to save certain animals. You may, or may not, think that his idea is a sound one.

Research Topics

1. Choose an animal and plan a campaign to save it.
2. Assess the animal's "public appeal," i.e. how to introduce the plight of the animal and interest people in helping.
3. Plan a variety of actions to make the plight of the animal known.
4. Make and motivate a list of public and industrial institutions which could help your campaign.

5

What do you think you'll be reading about
in this unit?

Partner Practice

WORD BUILDING

Here is another group of words with more than one form and use. You have learned at least one form of these words. Discuss as usual, and then use some of them to complete the sentences.

VERB	NOUN
manage	management
appoint	appointment
resent	resentment
retire	retirement
amuse	amusement
amaze	amazement
move	movement
enjoy	enjoyment
employ	employment

1. —I have to hurry. I'm late for an . . . .
   —So long. I've . . . ed seeing you.

2. —Do you need some help?
   —No thanks. I can . . . by myself.

3. —Was Anne surprised by your present?
   —Surprised! More than surprised—she was . . . d!

4. —How many people does your company . . . ?
   —Over 200.

5. —My wife has been . . . ed Personnel Manager!
   —Terrific! She must . . . her work.
   —Yes, she does. She says she's never going to . . . .

ON YOUR OWN

Work with a partner and make sentences of your own. Can you also use the *-ing* forms of the words in sentences?

Here's one more group of words to discuss and use in sentences.

VERB	ADJECTIVE	NOUN
confuse	confusing	confusion
satisfy	satisfying	satisfaction
construct	constructive	construction
imagine	imaginary	imagination
introduce	introductory	introduction
suspect	suspicious	suspicion
continue	continuous	continuation

1. —She tells fantastic stories, doesn't she?
   —Yes, she has quite an . . . .

2. —Have you finished the . . . of your house?
   —Yes, and it's a very . . . feeling.

3. —I don't understand this poem.
   —I don't either. It's very . . . .

4. —I want to . . . you to my friend, Tom.
   —Is he the jeweler you've talked about?
   —No, you have him . . . d with Jerry.

5. —I'm . . . of this ring. I don't think it's real.
   —Do you . . . somebody made a duplicate?
   —Yes. It would give me great . . . to catch the thief.

ON YOUR OWN

Work with a partner and make sentences of your own.
You can write some of them for extra credit.

Read & Predict

THE DISHONEST DESK CLERK

About a year ago, I registered at a Detroit hotel. I had just cashed a check. I didn't want to carry too much money with me, so I asked the desk clerk to put a hundred-dollar bill in the safe for me.

The next morning the clerk denied any knowledge of my money. I had neither a receipt nor any other proof that I had given the man my money. It was his word against mine. There was nothing I could do but go to the nearest lawyer.

The lawyer advised me to return to the hotel with him and give another hundred-dollar bill to the clerk. This we did. An hour later I went back to the desk and claimed my money. Since I had the lawyer as an eyewitness to the second hundred-dollar bill, the clerk could not look innocent and say he knew nothing about it.

Another hour later, I put the second part of the lawyer's plan into action. This time both the lawyer and I went to the hotel. I asked for the hundred-dollar bill, and when the clerk insisted he had already given it to me, I denied it. The lawyer said, "I saw this man give you a hundred dollars. If you don't hand it over immediately, I'll be forced to call the police." The clerk realized he had been tricked, but he knew he had to face the music. He gave me back the *first* hundred-dollar bill.

"I don't know how to thank you for getting my money back," I said to the lawyer. And what do you suppose he answered?

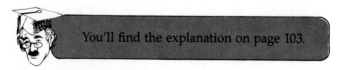

You'll find the explanation on page 103.

DO YOU REMEMBER?

1. When did the man stay in Detroit?
2. What did he ask the clerk to do?
3. Why did he have to go to a lawyer?
4. What was the first part of the lawyer's plan?

Partner Practice

Now use the pictures and words of your own to make more sentences. Be careful with the *do* and *does!*

Use the pictures and words of your own to make more sentences. Be careful with *am, is* and *are.*

—How do you know?
—Mother said so.

1. Is Jack going to help?
2. Will you pay for me?   hope
3. Do you know if he won?   am afraid
4. Is your dog sick?   I   believe   so.
5. Can you come to my party?   suppose
6. Will the weather be bad?   think

—Was he happy? (*be*)   —Was she happy too? (*suppose*)
—Yes, he was.   —Yes, I suppose so.

1. Did he hurt himself?(*be afraid*) 4. Is he satisfied?   (*be*)
2. Will she win?   (*hope*)   5. Do you know her?(*think*)
3. Did they succeed?   (*do*)   6. Are you certain? (*be*)

—Is she **rich**?
—I think so.
—Well, she **bought two cars,** didn't she?
—Oh, no. She's not **rich** enough to **buy two cars.**

1. brave/won a medal

2. talented/sang on TV

3. smart/learned Chinese

4. beautiful/won a
   beauty contest

THE DISHONEST DESK CLERK
The lawyer said, "Oh, don't thank me. That will be a hundred
dollars, please."

Read & Understand

THE CHEROKEE

Long before the white man came to the Americas, the land belonged only to the Indian. The Cherokee lived in what is now the southeastern part of the United States. They were peace-loving farmers who lived in permanent villages. They
5 built homes and public buildings of brick and stone. They had fine plantations.

When the first white men came, the Cherokee copied many of their ways. One Cherokee scholar, Sequoyah, saw how important reading and writing was to the white man. He
10 decided to make a written form of the spoken Cherokee language. At first he tried to make a sign, or symbol, for each word. But that proved impossible—there were just too many words. Then he took the 85 sounds that made up the Cherokee language. Using his own imagination and an English spelling
15 book, Sequoyah invented a sign for each sound. His alphabet proved amazingly easy to learn. Before long, many Cherokee knew how to read and write in their own language. By 1828, the Cherokee were even printing their own newspaper.

In 1830, the U.S. Congress passed a law. It said the
20 government could remove Indians from their lands. The Cherokee would not go. They had lived on their land for centuries. It belonged to them. Why should they go to a strange land far beyond the Mississippi River?

The army was sent to force the Cherokee out. Soldiers
25 surrounded their villages and marched them west at gunpoint. More than 4,000 Cherokee died during the terrible march. They called that march "The Trail of Tears." The end of the trail was also the end of the great Cherokee nation.

DO YOU REMEMBER?

1. Where did the Cherokee live?
2. Who was Sequoyah?
3. Why did he decide to invent an Indian alphabet?
4. Why wasn't it possible to have a sign for each word?
5. What did the Congress do in 1830?
6. What did the army do?
7. Why was the trip west called "The Trail of Tears?"

Listen & Understand

THE AUSTRALIAN ABORIGINES

1. Which picture shows an Australian Aborigine?

a.　　　　　　　　b.　　　　　　　　c.

2. Where did they find bootprints?

a.　　　　　　　　b.　　　　　　　　c.

3. Why couldn't the tracker follow the prints very far?

a.　　　　　　　　b.　　　　　　　　c.

4. Where was the wanted man hiding?

a.　　　　　　　　b.　　　　　　　　c.

5. Where do most of the Aborigines live?

a.　　　　　　　　b.　　　　　　　　c.

Partner Practice

—Hasn't the **wind** been **terrible** today?
—Yes, it's been **terribly windy.**

1. rain   awful

2. sun   wonderful

3. snow   amazing

4. fog   terrible

5. storm   unpleasant

6. ice   dreadful

—Does he always **drive so carelessly?**
—Yes, he's always been **a careless driver.**

1. **sing so loudly**
2. **dance so elegantly**
3. **walk so slowly**
4. **run so competitively**
5. **write so carefully**
6. **sleep so poorly**
7. **read so quickly**
8. **play so confidently**

How about you? What do you like or dislike?

| I | like
dislike | movies
plays
shows
concerts
stories
books
games
sports | that are
that end | boring.
exciting.
sad.
funny.
humorously.
interesting.
competitive.
unpleasantly.
amusing.
energetic.
sadly. |

| People can | answer
explain
listen
remember
speak | correctly, stubbornly
clearly, carefully, confidently
carelessly, angrily
loudly, reasonably
softly, quickly, slowly . . . |

—Did he give the **correct** answer?
—Yes, he answered **correctly.**

—Is he a **loud** speaker?
—Yes, he speaks very **loudly.**

—Did he give you a **clear** explanation?
—Yes, he explained **clearly.**

ON YOUR OWN

Practice making questions and answers like those above with your friend.

Read & Predict

LOST IN THE FOG

It's been quite some time since I was last in London, but something happened during that visit that I'll remember as long as I live. London is well-known for its terrible fogs. During my visit, it was terribly foggy.

It was even hard to see your hands. Cars and buses crept 5 along, their lights on and their horns blowing furiously. When evening fell, the weather got worse. All traffic came to a standstill. I had an important appointment on the other side of town that I couldn't put off. It was impossible to find a taxi; I decided it would be easier to walk. I set out confidently. 10

Minutes later I was completely lost. I couldn't even find a street sign to get my bearings. Then I heard a voice. "I suppose you are lost. Can I help you?" I could barely see the young woman who had spoken to me, but was grateful to find another person out in the fog. I explained where I wanted to 15 go, and she said she knew exactly how to get there. I was doubtful, but followed her through the dark streets.

The city seemed as quiet as a cemetery, and I remember thinking my guide could be leading me to an alley where she and some friends would rob me. But my fears were unfounded. 20 The woman led me right to my destination. I was amazed at how well she had found her way through the fog. "I know this part of town quite well," she replied. "But the fog—this terrible fog—made it impossible to see anything," I said.

 What do you suppose she answered? You'll find our explanation on page 113.

DO YOU REMEMBER?

1. What was the weather like?
2. Did it get better or worse during the day?
3. Why did he have to go out that evening?
4. Why did he decide to walk?
5. Did it take him long to get lost?
6. Who helped him?
7. Why was he afraid of the woman?
8. Did she have any trouble leading him to his destination?

Partner Practice

IDIOMS

Here are some idiomatic uses of **put**. Discuss and use in the sentences below.

put off	delay	Don't put off going to the dentist.
put in	spend time	I put in an hour of overtime.
put out	angry	I'm really put out with you.
put up to	get to do	Who put you up to that trick?
put up	build	They're going to put up a bank.
put up with	accept, allow	I won't put up with your behavior.
put down	criticize	Well, he really put down my idea.

1. —What's the matter? Why are you looking so . . . ?
   —I've been waiting an hour for you, that's why.

2. —I have to work late again tonight.
   —You . . . too much overtime.

3. —Do you think Mary resents me?
   —Yes. I don't know how you . . . her resentment.

4. —Weren't they going to . . . a school here?
   —Yes, but the construction has been . . . until next year.

5. —Why did you do that?
   —I didn't want to. Peter . . . me . . . it.

6. —I think my boss is unfair. He just . . . another idea of mine.
   —Well, I wouldn't . . . behavior like that.

ON YOUR OWN

Work with a partner. Make lists of things you sometimes *put off*, things that make you feel *put out*, and things you don't like to *put up with*.

IDIOMS

Here are some idiomatic uses of **look** to discuss and use.

look after	take care of	Please look after yourself.
look in on	visit	I'll look in on you tomorrow.
look over	check, read	Please look over this letter.
look up to	admire	I really look up to my uncle.
look up	find	Look up my friend Bill in Mexico.
look to	turn to for help	I just don't know who to look to.
look down on	have a low opinion of	I try not to look down on anybody.
look into	investigate	The police will look into the robbery.

1. —Would you check my paper for mistakes?
   —Sure. I can . . . it . . . this afternoon.

2. —Can you . . . the children? I have to go to the library.
   —What for?
   —To . . . some magazines on Peru.

3. —Why does Bill . . . John?
   —I don't know. His attitude is very unfair.

4. —The doctor will . . . you this afternoon.
   —Oh, thank you. He's so kind to visit me at home.

5. —Find out why Paul is so late.
   —I'll . . . it right away.

6. —When you need advice, who do you . . . ?
   —My grandfather. He's great. I really . . . him.

ON YOUR OWN

Work with a partner. Make lists of people you *look up to.*
Tell why you admire them so much.

Read & Understand

THE LAND IS OUR MOTHER

"The land is our Mother" is an Indian saying. In 1855, the United States government wanted to buy some Indian land. Chief Seathl of the Duwamish Tribe wrote this letter to the President of the United States.

5   The Great Chief in Washington sends word that he wishes to buy our land. We will think about your offer, for we know if we do not do so, the white man may come with guns and take our land. What Chief Seathl says the Great Chief in Washington can count on. My words are like the stars—they

10 do not set.

But how can they buy or sell the sky—the warmth of the land? The idea is strange to us. Yet we do not own the freshness of the air or the sparkle of the water. How can you buy them from us? We will decide in our time. Every part of

15 this earth is sacred to my people. Every tree, every sandy shore, every trail in the dark woods is holy in the memory and the experience of my people.

We know that the white man does not understand our ways. One part of the land is the same to him as the next.

20 He is a stranger who comes in the night and takes from the land whatever he needs. The earth is not his brother, but his enemy. His appetite will eat up the earth and leave behind only a desert.

Your cities pain the eyes of the red man. There is no quiet

25 place in the white man's cities. No place to hear the leaves of the spring or the sounds of birds' wings. The Indian prefers the soft sound of the wind, and the smell of the wind itself, cleaned by the rain. The air is precious to the red man, for all things share the same breath—the animals, the trees, and Man.

If we sell you our land, you must love it as we've loved it.   30
Care for it as we've cared for it. All things are connected.
Whatever happens to the earth, happens to the sons of the
earth. Preserve the land for your children, and love it as
God loves us all. One thing we know—our God is the same
God. The earth is precious to him. Even the white man cannot   35
remove himself from our common destiny.

DO YOU REMEMBER?

1. What does the Chief say will happen if he doesn't
   sell the land?
2. In what way can the Chief's words be counted on?
3. Why is the idea of selling the land strange to him?
4. How does he say the white man feels about the land?
5. How does he feel about the white man's cities?
6. If he sells the land, what does he want the white
   man to do?
7. What is a *prophet*? Can you call the Chief's words
   prophetic?
8. Think back to the reading in Unit 9 on the Cherokee
   Indians. What happened to their land? In what year?
   Do you think the experience of the Cherokee had an
   effect on Chief Seathl's words and feelings? Explain.

ON YOUR OWN

Pretend that you are Chief Seathl. You have gone
to Washington to talk about Indian problems with
the President. Make up a dialogue; act it out with
a partner in front of the class.

LOST IN THE FOG
"It makes no difference to me if it's foggy or clear. You see, I'm blind."

Listen & Understand

A SONG
You are going to hear a song by Suzanne Harris.

1. The title of the song is
   a. We're Helping the World
   b. We're Using Up the World
   c. We're Saving the World

2. The writer
   a. likes the way the earth is being used
   b. dislikes the way the earth is being used
   c. doesn't give an opinion

3. When men chopped down the tall trees, they
   a. left a big hole in the earth
   b. planted more trees
   c. left a big hole in the sky

4. Factories by the thousand are
   a. turning the rivers black
   b. turning out working men
   c. making it hard to make a living

5. The writer blames
   a. the government
   b. men in other countries
   c. all the people in the United States.

6. Wild animals are disappearing because
   a. they can't find enough to eat
   b. they're being killed for their coats
   c. they're being killed for food

7. What does Suzanne Harris want us to do?
   a. sing her song again
   b. tell a story told before
   c. preserve earthly things

ON YOUR OWN

How are the words of this song and Chief Seathl's words alike? What do you think about this?

Partner Practice

Can you complete each sentence so that
it makes good sense?

	hadn't met her before		couldn't speak it
	had looked at the map		well.
	had studied Spanish		were still hungry.
Although we	had eaten	we	got no answers.
			got lost.
	had tried hard		liked her at once.
	had sent three letters		didn't give up.
	had become tired		didn't win.

—He wasn't really rich.
—But did he have a chauffeur?
—Since he wasn't really rich, he couldn't
have a chauffeur, could he?

1. —He was very late.
   —But did he meet the train?
   —Since he was . . . .

2. —He was working in the barn.
   —But did he hear the telephone?
   —. . . .

3. —He fell asleep.
   —But did he see the end of the movie?
   —. . . .

4. —My brakes didn't work yesterday.
   —But did you drive anyway?
   —. . . .

5. —She lost my address.
   —But did she send you the tickets?
   —. . . .

6. —They both had terrible colds.
   —But did they sing well?
   —. . . .

Confessions of a Born Spectator

One infant grows up and becomes a jockey,
Another plays basketball or hockey,
This one the prize ring hastes to enter,
That one becomes a tackle or centre.
I'm just as glad as I can be
That I'm not them, that they're not me.

With all my heart do I admire
Athletes who sweat for fun or hire,
Who take the field in gaudy pomp
And maim each other as they romp;
My limp and bashful spirit feeds
On other people's heroic deeds.

Now A runs ninety yards to score;
B knocks the champion to the floor;
C, risking vertebrae and spine,
Lashes his steed across the line.
You'd think my ego it would please
To swap positions with one of these.

Well, ego might be pleased enough,
But zealous athletes play so rough;
They do not ever, in their dealings,
Consider one another's feelings,
I'm glad that when my struggle begins
Twixt prudence and ego, prudence wins.

When swollen eye meets gnarled fist,
When snaps the knee, and cracks the wrist,
When calm officialdom demands,
Is there a doctor in the stands?
My soul in true thanksgiving speaks
For this most modest of physiques.

Athletes, I'll drink to you or eat with you,
Or anything except compete with you;
Buy tickets worth their weight in radium
To watch you gambol in a stadium,
And reassure myself anew
That you're not me and I'm not you.

Ogden Nash

Fast Track: *Read and Research*

CASH FOR TRASH

A dilapidated garage in New York City's South Bronx would not be most people's idea of an office. But for Michael Schedler and his partners in Bronx 2000, a nonprofit development corporation, such an unlikely site became the first home eight years ago for a booming business: the R2D2 recycling plant.

"R2D2 started as a way to get garbage off the streets," explains Schedler, the plant's chief of operations. The trick was to pay people cash to bring in bottles, cans, newspapers and other trash. Soon, not only were the streets cleaner, but hundreds of the Bronx's disadvantaged residents had a steady source of income.

Today R2D2 has 30 employees and buys about 35 tons of nearly 30 different recyclable materials daily. The plant bales, melts, grinds or otherwise processes the discarded items and then sells them to companies for turning into new products.

A New York State law requiring stores to pay refunds on returned bottles and cans has taken away some of R2D2's business, but the facility, which will earn nearly $3 million in revenues this year, cannot begin to meet the demand for such materials as plastic and glass. Similar trash-taming plants have gone up in numerous cities, including Newark, Miami and Philadelphia.

NEW YORK

Michael Schedler's office is a dilapidated garage in New York City's South Bronx. The Bronx is one of the five boroughs of New York. The others are Manhattan, Brooklyn, Staten Island and Queens.

Research Topics

1. Where is New York City?
2. Who were the first settlers of New York?
3. Has New York always been called New York?
4. Has the ownership of the city changed hands through the years?
5. What is the New York of today like? What is it famous for?
6. What industries, schools, and places of interest are there in New York?

PRIVATE ENTERPRISE

Michael Schedler had an idea, worked on it and formed his own business. Today, his business is booming.

What would it be like to run your own business?

Research Topics

1. What different forms of companies exist?
2. How do you go about starting a business?
3. Are there any special restrictions?
4. Decide on a business. Try to think of something unique or suitable for you.
5. Determine how much capital you would need and where you would get the necessary financial backing.
6. Try to find suitable premises for your future business.
7. Consider the question of employing someone. What obligations does an employer have towards his or her employees?

RECYCLING

R2D2 was the name of the robot in the *Star Wars* films. Schedler named his recycling plant after the robot.

Just how much garbage do we produce each day? And how much are we wasting by not recycling more products?

Research Topics

1. Make an inventory of how much you throw away each day.
2. Make a list of how much you save for re-use every day.
3. Investigate what facilities your community has for recycling.
4. Suggest ways of facilitating recycling.
5. Examine products in your local store and report on which products are environment-friendly and which products are not suitable for recycling.
6. Compile evidence to show whether the costs of recycling are greater or smaller than the costs of living in a non-recycling consumer environment.

Index

Talking about:
ability, 103
ailments, 58
degree, condition, 82
existence/availability, 26–27, 30
hope, 38, 51
how things are done, 107
inventions, 15
job-related topics, 17
measurement, 59
past/recent past action, 2, 3
personal information, 107
recent activities, 31
Weather expressions, 106

Listening Comprehension

9, 17, 33, 41, 57, 65, 81, 89, 105, 114

Reading Comprehension

4, 8, 12, 16, 22–24, 28, 36, 40,
46–48, 52, 56, 60, 64, 70–72,
76, 80, 84, 88, 94–96, 100, 104,
108, 112, 118–120

Content Reading

Environmental issues:
endangered species, 94–96
recycling, 118–120
industrial pollution, 70–72
tree restoration, 22–24
tropical forest devastation,
46–48

Literature

20–21, 44–45, 68–69, 92–93,
116–117

Pronunciation

Homonyms, 79
Silent letters, 18
Stress/syllabication, 111

Writing

Guided assignments, 18, 67, 78
79, 86, 87, 91, 98, 99, 102 110,
111, 113
Independent assignments, 23–24,
47–48, 70–71, 95–96, 119–120